Maro

A childhood in Cyprus and a life beyond

By

Maria Norwell

MAPLE
PUBLISHERS

Maro (A Childhood in Cyprus and A Life Beyond)

Author: Maria Norwell

Copyright © Maria Norwell (2023)

The right of Maria Norwell to be identified as author of this work has been asserted by the author in accordance with section 77 and 78 of the Copyright, Designs and Patents Act 1988.

First Published in 2023

ISBN 978-1-915492-87-6 (Paperback)
  978-1-915492-88-3 (Hardback)
  978-1-915492-89-0 (E-Book)

Book cover design and Book layout by:
  Maple Publishers
  www.maplepublishers.com

Published by:
  Maple Publishers
  Fairbourne Drive
  Atterbury
  Milton Keynes
  MK10 9RG
  www.maplepublishers.com

This is a tale of history and stories, of how what you are told of your past and what you live through becomes your future – you make your own legacy to pass on and this is mine. While my children and grandchildren may have already heard much of my story, there are many generations to come and I want to tell them, this is what you came from, this is what runs through your blood. *Be proud of it – and always look for the whole of the moon.*

My story is of what it means to be a strong woman with a fighting spirit, to have a passion for life and the will to always strive for a legacy that will mean something. But my story is also a bridge between two different worlds, what was expected of the generation before me and the start of the new one I would inhabit.

It is a story of a child who experienced so much, and of the woman she became – it is a story of life, and of always striving for more. It is the story of a little girl called Maro...

Prologue

Cyprus is an ancient country of myths and legends. When I was a young girl it was also a place of secrets and contradictions with sincerely held religious beliefs co-existing with superstition and a lingering hint of witchcraft. Education and freedom were for boys; duty, chastity and obedience for girls. My own family and upbringing were exceptional in that my mother was educated and my parents came from opposite ends of the social spectrum.

We all have snapshots of our lives, moments which stay with us or times which, on reflection, seem so momentous even if they were ordinary when they occurred. When I think back over my life, my mind always travels to the little girl I was – to little Maro. She swims in the bright blue waters of her youth, she climbs the hills of her village, she runs and plays and is welcomed by everyone who meets her. She is a child of freedom and pleasure.

I was such a happy child – and it is easy to see why. I had so much. I lived in paradise, I was strong and I was determined. I always wanted to be someone and I never doubted that would happen. It was my destiny, but it was also something I could work towards. That little girl was building the foundations of the life which would be mine.

And what would I say to her now? What would I say to that child? I would tell her to be herself, to strive for all she could in life. I would urge her to enjoy what she had for as long as it lasted and to always be the best version of herself. I would encourage her to take the hardships of life which were coming her way and to overcome them as best she could, even when they seemed insurmountable.

I would wrap her in my arms and warn her that there would be difficulties ahead, heart-breaking, terrible events, but that she was strong and she would overcome them all. I would tell her that she was a force of nature and that she should reach for the moon – and be proud of everything she did in life and all she became.

We all have a story to tell, and this is hers – this is mine.

Contents

Chapter One

Y ou cannot know your own story unless you know the story of those who made you – which is why I want to tell mine. It is a strange thing to put together the past of the people who went before you, especially, that of your parents. Much of what I know about both my mother and father comes from snatches of conversation overheard when I was a child, gossip and rumour that I listened to when I wasn't even meant to be there. At other times, I was perhaps perceived as just a little girl playing by the fire as the women chatted, not realising that, while my mouth was closed, my ears were very much open. I devoured all of these stories, all of the pieces which allowed me to build up a picture of how my parents came to be who they were and, as a result, how I came to be who I am.

Most of the stories about Father's past unspooled slowly. His origins were almost mythical in our family and they showed a life of incredible contradictions. His name was Kypros and he was the middle child of three. Papa had two siblings, an older sister called Irene, and a younger brother named Nicolas.

Kypros' family lived ten miles or so west of Kyrenia in a village called Lapithos, and they survived on very little. Their mother, Eleni, was an extremely beautiful woman – she was five feet six inches tall, slim and shapely, with fair hair and large almond shaped hazel eyes, all of which made her very attractive. It was her beauty which had been the source of many of her problems.

Before her children were born, Eleni had worked in fields belonging to a man called Postanos, a nickname given to him meaning 'someone with property'. Postanos was the father of Irene and Kypros, but he had his own family who also lived in the village. He wanted nothing to do with his illegitimate son and daughter, giving no emotional or financial support whatsoever. It was quite uncommon to be illegitimate in those days and very much frowned upon. Eleni was left with the children as her responsibility, with no input from Postanos who simply ignored her and their children.

The first time I heard Papa mentioning the name of his own father was when I was about ten years old. I overheard him telling my mother that Postanos was considering recognising Papa officially as his son – this never went ahead as my father's half-brother, the legitimate son of Postanos, would not allow it. I remember Papa being so disappointed. I also remember it being one of the few times any reference was made to his past at all. He never spoke about his upbringing and childhood, all I have is what I gleaned from those eavesdropped conversations, especially those between Mama and Auntie Irene.

There is actually only one story that I directly recall him telling Mama which was about an old teacher from his school being taken to the local sanatorium as he had TB. Father gave this man a lift and, from the front seat of the car heard the man say to himself, 'Indeed how strange it is and how ironic that one of my worst ever pupils is carrying me on my last journey.' I am getting ahead of myself here, for the fact that Papa was a terrible student is part of the story of who he was and the life he led as a child.

Kypros and Irene were very alike in looks, the brother and sister both fair-haired and golden, both with green-blue eyes, with sunburned complexions, but when their little brother, Nicolas arrived, it was clear that they did not share the same father. Nicolas was a great deal darker, with almost black hair and sallow skin; the father of this child was obviously not Postanos. The paternity of Nicolas was actually reputed to be that of a monk from the nearby monastery of Acheiropoietos who, again, provided nothing for his child.

Eleni now had three illegitimate children and could only rely upon herself to provide for them. Living in one room attached to a stable, they had very little – nothing more than rags and dirty faces. They would play by the stream with only their imaginations, trying to ignore their empty stomachs and trying to avoid wondering whether there would be any food on the table that evening. Often Eleni would spend the day looking for scraps, scouring the fields for anything that was edible, or going from house to house, trying to sell a handful of figs she had managed to pick from the one and only fig tree towering over the small yard in front of their one room home.

Attached to that room was another room belonging to Eleni's sister Eugenia. Beyond Eugenia's place, there was a little stable with goats and hens that ran about all over the front yard and field. Eugenia also lived on her own with her two boys, her husband having left after their sons were born. Unlike Eleni, Eugenia had not been blessed with beauty. She was small and dark, with uneven features, stooped over, almost witch-like. I think back to these women and realise how much they had to fight to survive. None of the men who had fathered their children provided for them, all three left their duties behind in one way or another. And yet the women kept going, doing what little they could, but never running away from their responsibilities.

I would like to know more of Eleni, and Eugenia, but they are not the ones who determine where my life will go in this tale, so let us go back to the little boy who would become my father.

Kypros was very intelligent. From an early age, he took it upon himself to provide for his mother and siblings by doing little errands and working in the fields. Going to school was a luxury they couldn't afford. It is difficult to attend and learn on an empty stomach which meant that Father never really went to school. You have to have food before you can have education. You need to feed a child before that child can learn. That sort of life did not sit well with the dreams and ambitions of Kypros. He was only nine years old when he left home and there are two versions to the story. The first one - which I heard from my mother - is that Kypros managed to get on a boat heading for Palestine, where he discovered that he had to pay for his passage by scrubbing the decks. He was a hardworking boy and had a good, outgoing personality – as well as being very handsome – and all of this contributed to his rise. In Palestine, he tried to survive by doing little jobs such as shoe shining, jobs of low status but enough that he survived. One day, by chance, a British high-ranking official encountered him. He immediately saw the potential of this little boy and took him under his care. The name of this saviour and guardian was Sir Arthur J Lawe who was Deputy Undersecretary to the Colonies during the 1940s.

The other version of the story, which I heard later, was that Kypros got himself to Nicosia, the capital of Cyprus, by walking barefoot over the Pentadaktylos mountains. There he wandered the streets, trying to survive by sleeping rough even though it was wintertime, with stormy and very cold conditions. Kypros sheltered from the elements under a big doorway which was the home of Sir Arthur J Lawe, Cyprus being a British colony at that time.

Sir Arthur Lawe felt sorry for the little boy and asked his servant to bring him into the house where he was given dry clothes to wear, food to eat and a bed to sleep in. Whichever version of the story is to believed, there are common threads. Kypros was very grateful to Sir Arthur and promised that he would try hard to please him by becoming a useful member of the household. As he was a responsive and quick learner he soon picked up the English language, which as an adult he could speak like a native with an Oxford accent that mirrored Sir Arthur.

Kypros assumed more and more responsibilities and eventually took charge of his guardian's household. My father was brought up in the English culture and ways, all of which were very different from his life in the village of Lapithos and the little bothy where he had slept, always hungry and often cold. From what I heard, the fact that Kypros was blessed with good looks, appearing more Anglo Saxon than the locals, stood very much in his favour. His fair hair, bright blue-green eyes, and reddish sunburnt complexion combined with the fact that he grew tall and strong with a pleasant, outgoing personality. I wish I knew more of Papa's life during those years – all I do know is that, by the time he reached his twenties, he was indispensable to the man who had saved him. It was at this time that Sir Arthur was appointed as the head of The Pacific and Mediterranean and East Africa Departments of the UK Colonial Office (1936 – 1939). Kypros took his place as his right-hand man. My father travelled extensively with him over the next three or four years to Palestine, Cairo, Egypt, and more. The whole of the Middle East became their stomping ground, as all were colonies under British rule.

However, these places were not without their dangers. There was an uprising in Palestine and an attacker targeted Sir Arthur. Kypros protected him, shooting the attacker who would have undoubtedly killed his mentor. Sir Arthur had saved him from the grip of poverty and now Kypros had saved him from his would-be assassin. The relationship between the two men became even stronger. Kypros very soon learned the Arabic language as he seemed to have a gift for learning languages and was now trilingual, again proving himself to be indispensable.

Many miles back in Cyprus, another story was beginning to unfold. It was a stormy night, the wind was howling, the rain was lashing on the window panes. Everybody was running for shelter out of the storm as it was easy to believe that the world was coming to an end. A few miles from Lapithos, a young woman in her twenties sat alone, reading a book as the storm raged, her family asleep in other rooms in the large house. This woman, Kassandra Kalava, was attractive and intelligent, and had just qualified as a teacher. Her family was wealthy and she had a bright future ahead of her. Who knows why she could not sleep through the storm like the rest of them? However, if she had, my story would not be the one it is today.

Over the noise of the stormy turmoil outside, she heard a loud *thud, thud, thud* on the front door. *Who was it in this weather, at this hour, wandering in the storm*? she asked herself.

Kassandra approached the door with trepidation – there could be anyone out there. When she opened it, her fear dissipated as she found a peasant woman dressed in the usual garb of the town, a black skirt with a shawl over her head and down to her knees. This woman was absolutely drenched at the doorway, asking for shelter. She was lost, very distressed and Kassandra was a kind and caring young woman who didn't hesitate before asking the woman inside.

She scampered about, looking for some dry clothing for the woman to change into and sat her by the fireplace. She then looked for something she could give her to eat as she was starving. The storm continued relentlessly and Kassandra knew that she couldn't possibly send this poor woman out there again into the howling wind and rain. It was very dark, her home in Lapithos was at least a couple of miles away and she could easily get lost. Kassandra told the grateful woman that she would happily give her a bed for the night and hopefully the weather would be better in the morning.

As the night went on, she chatted a great deal to Kassandra telling her about her son, a clever, handsome boy who lived abroad. She showed the young woman his photograph which she carried at all times as she was extremely proud of him. Kassandra became very interested, he was indeed very good looking and about the same age as her . . .

The woman went on to tell her that her son was in Palestine temporarily, achieving great success working for the Governor. When he came back in a few months, she would certainly arrange a meeting between them, she was sure that they would like each other and who knows what might happen?

The woman was Eleni, my grandmother.

Her son was my father Kypros.

The young woman was my mother.

Grandmother Eleni (as she would become) kept her promise and, after a few months, Kypros returned to Cyprus where the introduction took place. He was indeed very handsome as Kassandra had been told, over six feet tall, slim, mannerly and charming. The attraction was mutual and he was delighted with the beautiful, intelligent young woman who had sheltered his mother from the storm. It was clear that the two were meant for each other and they soon declared their plans to marry.

However, Kassandra faced many difficulties when she presented her new love. Her relatives refused to accept Kypros into the family. Lapithos, where Kypros was from, was very close to Karavas and word travels fast.

'This man does not have a suitable background,' Kassandra was told. 'A leopard cannot change its spots and a man born into poverty will return there.'

Kassandra was adamant. She had fallen in love with Kypros at first sight and was absolutely determined that this was the man she wanted to marry.

'His background does not matter to me,' she would reply. 'Only our future together. He is a man who has already done great things and he is the husband I am determined to have.' Kassandra's opinion was of no concern to many in her family, especially those who saw themselves in a position of power and felt they had the right to determine the wishes of others, especially women.

Ophelia was Kassandra's older sister by ten years, and she was already married to a man called Alexander who was older than her by a good few years. They had a family of their own but Alexander also considered himself the guardian of Kassandra. He was determined that a union such as that with Kypros would not happen. Alexander was a teacher, quite a big man, black hair, sallow skin and bulging eyes. He was not good looking and had an extreme, authoritarian personality which overshadowed everything else about him.

Every time my mother repeated that she wanted to marry my father, Alexander would repeat his own words too. 'You cannot marry a man like him with that kind of background – you must be crazy. It doesn't matter if you are in love with him. Come on, you are not in your right senses Kassandra.'

There was no denying that Kypros did indeed come from a very poor background and background was all-important to someone like Alexander, and to many others. His being the illegitimate son of a landless peasant woman made him totally unsuitable to marry into their family. The family into which Alexander had married was prosperous and enjoyed high status in the community. They mixed with similar families, and they could be ruthless in their scorn for those who transgressed the rigid rules of their class. Many within Kassandra's family were jealous of how successful Kypros had become. As he went on to become a successful businessman their resentment did not diminish and becoming a wealthier man through his own effort did not endear him to the old families. On the contrary, the more successful he became, the more jealous they became and they never truly accepted him because of his background.

Kassandra made up her own mind and nobody could change it. She stood up to Alexander and everyone who said the union would never work, soon getting engaged to Kypros and then marrying him. She was told by so many people of how terrible it was to bring the name of the family down, in an almost unforgivable way but she stood firm.

The newlyweds moved into the family compound which they shared with Kassandra's parents. This was a traditional country home, extending in all directions with an outdoor oven and multiple yards with raised vines above them. I suspect this was not an ideal situation given the respective strong personalities of all parties and it caused yet more resentment from the wider family with the expectation that Kypros and Kassandra would remain in the ancestral home when her parents passed on. Communications with many other members of the family had now stopped altogether.

All of this is a prelude to my origins. I come from a long line of strong, resilient characters. Nothing would trip them up or stop them, they pushed on and on, whether that was my mother determining her own marriage in a way which was unusual back then, or my paternal grandmother raising her children in poverty but somehow instilling in my father the will to fight his way out of that life. The manner in which he made his own way in the world and the way in which he and my mother were determined that their love would win, are all indicators of what runs through my veins – the spirit and the heart, the soul and the determination.

Chapter Two

My sister Chrysoula was born a year after my parents' wedding and then two years down the line, I came along. I was born at home in the early hours of a Monday morning with the help of a midwife (or mammou). It was apparently a natural birth but a difficult one. In those days, women wore a corset or binder postnatally to keep themselves constricted and prevent them from expanding in all directions. Apparently, Mama wouldn't wear one of these binders since the time of my birth – the 11th of August – was during a very hot time of the year, when temperatures could reach one hundred degrees Fahrenheit. Mama always complained that because it was too hot for her to wear such a thing, people thought that she was overweight – and that it was my fault for deciding to arrive during the summer.

I had a large extended family around me and the whole of the village to make a fuss of little Maro as I was known. My mother had my brother Nicolas a year or so after I was born but, sadly, he died when he was one. My next brother, Thomas, who was conceived soon after, died at 18 months when I was about three years of age. Both of my baby brothers were thought to have died of pneumonia. This may indeed have been the direct cause of their deaths but it later transpired that there was a family genetic disposition to ATRX Syndrome (Alpha-thalassemia x-linked intellectual disability syndrome). This syndrome is defined as *a genetic condition that causes intellectual disability, muscle weakness (hypotonia), short height, a particular facial appearance, genital abnormalities, and possibly other symptoms.* This condition is transmitted by the female line of the family and manifests in the males, a little like the better known haemophilia. It was something which ran through the family, not just in terms of the boys who sadly died, but in the minds and fears of everyone. Why did so many of the boys not survive? Why did so many of them succumb to pneumonia or other infections, while the girls were healthy?

I remember the day Thomas died. A crowd of village women, all dressed in black from head to toe, swarmed through the house. One or two of them took it upon themselves to keep an eye on me and prevent me entering the room, or indeed the house, where my infant brother was lying dead in his cot with my mother by his side. I was convinced that something awful was going on. Of course, something awful *had* happened, but as a small child, I must have thought that my mother had been taken from me as I wasn't allowed to see her.

Several times, I tried to escape from the women's stranglehold but without success.

'Little girls are not allowed in the house,' I was told repeatedly. 'Your mother is very busy.'

I kept asking questions but none was answered. I wondered where my sister Chrysoula was – she was two years older than I and she should have been around but was nowhere to be seen either. Perhaps she was more successful in entering the house. I still don't know and we never spoke of it.

I became very uneasy sitting on the stone wall separating one of the courtyards from the garden. The medlar tree was towering above with its long, oval striated leaves, bowed with yellow fruit. It must have been the beginning of April or May as I remember that yellow fruit well. Eventually the crowd of women disappeared and I realised after some time that my angelic little baby brother was nowhere to be seen. I very much doubt that anyone would have thought to sit down and explain things to me. I would have been glad to see Mama, and the absence of Thomas eventually worked its way into my consciousness, but an awareness of what had happened would only come with time. At that time, it was often thought that young children should not be exposed to death and it was almost certainly with kind intent that I was kept in the dark.

Our house was set deep amongst lemon and orange groves in the middle of Karavas. The house was covered with greenery and climbing plants, especially at the back to keep it cool in the hot summer months. I lived in the sun, in idyllic surroundings and surrounded by nature. It was like Paradise – mostly.

I must have only been a toddler when, seated on my mother's knee under our Virginia Creeper covered veranda, the beginning of my lifelong terror of caterpillars began. It gradually developed into a fear of all creepy crawlies but on that day started when a very large caterpillar fell on me from the creeper above. I would probably have thought nothing of it but Mama, unfortunately being phobic of them herself, screamed and made a great deal of fuss. I knew that my fear and behaviour was irrational, but it made no difference. The more I tried, the worse I felt as I got older. We had no clinical psychologists to help with such problems in those days, so I continued to be plagued with such fears for years to come, especially in my disturbed dreams. I think the dropping caterpillar is probably my first memory, and one which is seared into my mind.

I was an alert, active child who had apparently started to walk at the age of nine months. I was interested in everything according to my mother, being inquisitive and enquiring about all things around me. I have a few memories just after the caterpillar incident, probably from when I was around 18 months of age.

One such memory is of a huge rat caught in a large cage in the fields. My maternal grandmother - or 'Stete' as I called her - took me by the hand and I tiptoed over to look at it.

'I think it would be best if I poured boiling water over this creature. That will kill it, that will do the trick. What do you think Maro?' she asked.

I had absolutely no idea what to think! I couldn't tear my eyes away from this enormous creature in front of us and I was delighted when Mama appeared to decide that I shouldn't even be there.

'What a thing to suggest!' she exclaimed. 'Maro doesn't need to see such things – come with me,' she declared, taking me by the hand and snatching me away from the scene.

On another occasion, a black adder – which must have been about three metres in length - was found, again by my grandmother, in the irrigation ditch just above the front yard of the house in the field of Uncle Panayiotis. She didn't disturb it but told me stories of how it was a 'farmer's friend' as it was so good at catching and eating rats.

There were quite a few poisonous snakes around and many tales to go with them. When my mother was pregnant with me, she was using the outdoor toilet – rather indelicately I have to say she was in a squatting position. As she sat there, a large snake came through the window of the toilet, over onto the ceiling, dropping onto the toilet. She was quite righty terrified. These creatures were everywhere.

Chrysoula, my older sister, was asked one lunchtime to bring some bay leaves from the garden for the barbeque and on one of the branches was a snake, wound along it, waiting. She was lucky not to be bitten, because she saw it in time, but was scarred with a fear of snakes from that moment. Mother kept an antidote for snake bites in the kitchen in one of the cupboards as we never knew when one might appear. The antidote was a small, mottled baby snake in a bottle of mixed olive oil and vinegar which, thankfully, we never had to use, but the threat was always there.

When I was older, Chrysoula and I were left to entertain ourselves whilst Mama was in the fields and father at work. One summer day. Chrysoula was convinced that she saw a big snake in the pantry. We both panicked and ran to one of our neighbours, who was a farmer. He came along to look for it with his enormous spade, but the snake escaped and was not to be found. A missing snake was just as worrying to me! These were themes which ran throughout my childhood, but the presence of snakes, rats and whatever else were just the price to pay for living in a land so rich with nature. For me, the association of my homeland with many phobias was a deep one, but it was also just the other side of the coin of having such a wonderful world on my doorstep.

My people had lived in Karavas for centuries. Karavas was a beautiful place lying in the valley between the Pentadaktylos (meaning the mountain of five peaks in the shape of a hand with five fingers) and the sea. We stayed in the middle of the village, equidistant to both the sea and the mountain. It was such a privilege to be able to enjoy both, although as a child you simply accept your life not knowing whether it is special or not. As I grew older, we often climbed the mountain especially in winter and spring when it was cooler. St George's Chapel, carved out of the rocks, was a frequent destination of ours, accessible only by a narrow pathway at the side of the mountain. We would get up at 4 or 5 am and climb up the steep slope to the Chapel, light a candle and return home. It didn't matter how many times we went, we always enjoyed it. There were pink, blue and white anemones, wild cyclamen from the end of winter in February, and a variety of mountain flowers throughout the year which we would gather to take back home.

During the hot summer days, we would go to the sea, swim in the cool blue water, often have lunch, then enjoy the sea breeze before walking back up to the village. Sometimes, if lucky, one of the bus drivers would stop to give us a lift back in a 'Tsentas' or 'Kallis', a local village bus. The whole of Northern Cyprus, now Turkish occupied, was beautiful and Karavas was not an exception. The main disadvantage of it was its proximity to Turkey. Just opposite our coast, about forty miles away, was the Turkish plain of Antalya and the Taurus Mountain. In winter, when the Taurus Mountain was covered with snow, bitterly cold winds would blow our way and the surface of the water was covered with a layer of ice. Occasionally, the odd fisherman would lose his way and get shot by the Turks. This had happened to a young man from the village who was just twenty years old.

On the right of the bay was Lambousa, one of the Seven Kingdoms of ancient Cyprus. The name means bright and shining because of its gold and wealth. This is where the people of Karavas village used to live prior to moving further inland avoid the attacks of the invaders. For me, it was a place we went to for picnics. Amongst the ruins of Lambousa was a large football pitch and there was plenty of space to run about and play ball games. On one of these excursions, I learned my first English words by counting through the song 'One man and his dog, went to mow a meadow'.

This was where I was raised, a place of beauty and nature, of serenity and enjoyment. When I look back on my childhood, it is hard to identify at what age I became aware of everything which surrounded me as it was always there. The walks and the picnics, the swimming and the exploration – awareness was incremental as it was all so natural. I cannot really say, *I did this when I was two*, or *I went here when I was three*, for everything just blended into everything else most of the time, one wonderful day after another.

Our house was an old traditional folk house with arches and originally with a cobbled floor, passed down from generation to generation. It was surrounded by productive orchards and gardens with all sorts of fruit trees – banana, lemon, plum, orange, tangerine, grapefruit, pomegranate, walnut, guava, medlar, almond and tall palm trees. It was the Garden of Eden and I lived a magnificent life with so much available to me. At the front of the fruit garden there were lots of flowering bushes separated from the house by a long low wall on which there were dozens of flowerpots which had to be watered daily during summer. I particularly liked the cacti pots especially when in bloom. I was, however, very disappointed when the cacti flowers would only last for twenty-four hours after so much anticipation. Despite that, their aroma and beauty were amazing. I retain such a vivid image of them growing at the side of our backyard on the right of the wall. There was also a large pot of 'Erotas', the love plant with its thorny branches, small oval green leaves and tiny red flowers. This 'Erotas' guarded the back gate to our house.

At the front of the house, beyond the yard, there was a high stone wall and above and beyond it was my uncle's lemon and fruit orchard which was bordered by the river. The river was stony, deep, with high banks in places and waterfalls during the winter months – now and again it would flood and on one occasion when I was still very young, the water came my uncle's field, down the wall and into the house, which was terrifying. The same river (a seasonal one which we called Arkhachi river) completely dried up during summer with only a trickle of water during spring. On one occasion a terrible accident occurred on the riverbed. The local fisherman had illegally hidden small balls of gunpowder which he used for fishing. These were found by a group of neighbourhood young boys – they exploded and maimed some of children.

At certain times of the year, there were eels and frogs in the pools of the riverbed which were very tempting to us all but we were not allowed to play there at any time except with adult supervision, especially after the accident with the boys. On the other side of the river spread the neighbourhood of Petroyitonia which meant 'the stony neighbourhood'. Just after Easter, on what was known as 'swing day', the boys living in the two small flat roof houses beyond the river embankment would put up a large swing, tying its thick ropes on the branches of a large tree. The four ropes would be attached at either end of a long thick board. The swing could take four or five people at a time with two of the boys standing either end propelling the swing backwards and forwards. It was the highlight of the year for me, the boys would give us all their attention, very pleased that my sister and I had condescended to cross the river to join in the fun. This was an exceptional annual event and otherwise we were never allowed to cross over to the other side. We would stay on the other side for hours having lots of fun with the children of the neighbourhood. When the sun came down, exhausted but happy, we would return back home until the next Easter. The boys acted as strangers to us, as we were to them, for the rest of the year.

Our house was a two-storey building. The ground floor had three large bedrooms, a bathroom, sitting room, dining kitchen and substantial storeroom full of big barrels of oil, with storage for halloumi, olives, flour, potatoes, tomatoes, onions and all the vegetables for day-to-day use. Beyond the storeroom there was a large room from which there was access from the side yard. The side yard had vines above it, raised on stilts and eventually tapered into a path which also had overhanging vines. The path led to my grandmother's olive grove and to the stables for her many animals, such as donkeys, goats and hens.

Occasionally my grandparents stayed in this last room; when my grandfather, (Pappous) suffered a stroke they were there for a while as my mother looked after him during the stressful recovery period. He must have been about eighty years of age, his brain was functioning relatively well and he had his speech so I guess it must have been a left-side stroke. Stroke patients were looked after in a completely different way back then. Once afflicted with the problem they were nursed in bed, they were not encouraged to be up and about or relearning how to walk and live life independently. It was indeed very difficult for the carers – my poor mother was very stressed at the time having to look after not only my Pappous but her own children and the workers gathering the produce from the fields (lemons, olives, carobs and almonds). She was hardworking, able and appeared to be coping very well considering everything, but it must have been a tremendous burden. When she became pregnant with her fifth surviving child (Thea), she was employed at Amiandos as a teacher. At that point, she decided to stop teaching and devote her life to the family and the management of the household .

I think that, because there was so much to do, a willing child such as I was always going to be encouraged to help. As soon as I was old enough to go for errands, my mother considered me the best candidate to go to the foot of the mountain and fetch her a box of tiny silkworms. Despite my caterpillar phobia, I was thought to bestow luck on her crop. She would nurture the silk worms and feed them every day on mulberry leaves until they became enormous white caterpillars with a black spot for a mouth. We all had to help bring the mulberry branches from one of our fields further down the village for them to feed upon. It was quite an onerous task every day, especially as the caterpillars became bigger and bigger and, as a result, were consuming a considerable amount of food. A couple of large racks were raised on stilts, stretching the length of one of the rooms in the garage, and our yearly lodgers could be heard munching away on the leaves until they grew large, climbed on thyme and other aromatic branches we provided for them before becoming a cocoon. As I grew older and my phobia escalated I refused to collect mother's precious box from the peasant woman on the hill or to enter the silkworm room, but she continued to be preoccupied by them despite the fact I was no longer willing to bring her luck with her crop.

I distinctly remember one morning prior to my father leaving for work holding in his hand one of the overfed caterpillars and trying a version of his own desensitisation for my fear. He entreated me to touch the object of my phobia and if I did, I was promised a pound in return. I was well aware from a young age of the value of money and a pound was a lot of money in those days. I very much wanted to have it for my piggy bank which so far was full of mostly pennies. It didn't matter how much I tried that morning – after a step or two forward, I would pull back. 'One step forward, two steps back', as the song goes. Eventually my father gave up. The strange thing was that I didn't mind helping with the final product, the cocoons, taking the fluffy silky thread off them, but the actual creatures? No thank you!

Although trivial in retrospect, these events were quite traumatic at the time. There were other truly serious events which made such a deep impression on me that I remember every second of them to this day. Although still so small, it was around this time that I was to be exposed to one of the most traumatic events of my life.

Front entrance of my parent's house

Me, my parents, sister Chrysoula, and baby brother, Andreas

On the veranda with Chrysoula

Chapter Three

Superstition was strong in my early childhood and when things went wrong, people often resorted to folklore. Desperate times make people act in desperate ways and this was the case for my mother. After she had me, my parents were desperate for a boy. Boys were what mattered – girls were all very well and good, but a boy was the goal. For my mother, although she had given birth to sons, they had not survived. She had lost two after me and was extremely upset about it. Not only was she grieving for the babies she had lost, she was also grieving for the lack of an heir and someone who would carry on the family name.

There was a woman who lived in the middle of the village who often visited Mama. This wasn't unusual in itself as mother was very generous and open with people. My father was generally away at work and she used to have a lot of people coming into the house as she was left to her own devices. The house was big and many people passed through it, some of them quite needy, looking for my mother's help and she was generous with them. She would give food and advice, and sometimes I suspect she gave them a little money.

These people were clearly in need of her, they required support and she was always willing to give that. She also felt obliged to feed the poor because of her religious beliefs. There was definitely a moral aspect to her aid.

There was one woman (Erato) who came every morning to go through the newspaper with her. Mama would read it and they would discuss politics and suchlike as Mama was very interested in political issues. This particular woman used to annoy me, she would talk a lot and she wasn't particularly nice to the rest of us, only interested in our mother. I think Mama needed company herself and she indulged Erato.

We used to visit another woman from further up the village, Eftyhia. She had a son who lived abroad. She would tell my mother what she wanted written in a letter, which Mama would write, and the young man would reply from Britain. I would listen into these conversations, wondering where the story would go, although nothing terribly exciting ever happened. Eftyhia unfortunately had a stroke so our visits for letter-writing stopped. Although we continued to visit her, she was a unable to communicate by then.

Some of these visitors played a much bigger role in our lives. There was another woman called Panayiota who would go about the village with a big bundle of goods. She would carry needles, clothes, fabric, all sorts of things and people would buy them when she went to their door. Sometimes my mother would buy something or give her some soup. On one occasion when my sister Chrysoula was very, very young, just a baby, there was an issue with her christening linen.

The white clothes of a christening need to be washed carefully and respectfully after the baptism, and the water in which they are rinsed cannot be poured down the drain. When the white christening gown is washed for the first time, it is holy, indicating purity, and cannot be poured down a drain but has to be put around plants to make them grow. This ritual usually fell to the godparents. Chrysoula's godfather was a doctor who lived in Nicosia, about 18 miles from us. When it became time to wash the linen, this godfather was too far away to travel for the rite and he would not have done it anyway being a man.

Panayiota was passing by one day and my mother started discussing the whole christening linen situation with her.

'I don't know what we will do with the christening linen,' she said. 'There is no one to deal with it.'

'Oh, that is easy,' Panayiota replied. 'I will do it.'

Indeed, she did and after that she was, by definition, Chrysoula's godmother as she had been part of the process. Given an alternative, I do not think the offer would have been accepted. Panayiota had been married at one point but had an acrimonious divorce. Her ex-husband used to deal with wells and he visited our house one day when Panayiota was there. We had a well in one of the back yards which was extremely deep. You could look inside but it went down to nowhere, you would just see a sparkle of water at the end of it. This man came to do some work to it. In order to go down, he needed a rope with a special mechanism. The rope was wound around a special reel and it was something he had obviously done many times before, to get to the bottom of wells. When Panayiota realised that he was doing this, she wanted to loosen the rope and drown him! My mother had a terrible problem to get her away from the well.

When Panayiota became really ill, my mother used to send Chrysoula and me, still very small girls, up to the foot of the mountain to give her food. As a divorcee with no children, she had no-one to care for her. We'd walk into the room, a gloomy, dark place, with a little passage right in the middle stacked with all sorts of things she had collected over the years. Panayiota had a little bed in the corner and I remember going up to her to give her the food and really being very frightened. Eventually when she became too ill, my mother brought her to stay in one of the rooms at the back of our house so she could look after her. Mama was kind, she would do things for many people but that seemed too much to me.

When Panayiota died, Chrysoula, being her godchild, inherited the little house. Despite its size and gloomy ambience. It turned out to be worth £800 which was an awful lot of money then. It allowed Chrysoula to start well in life and that had just come from mother being kind to a woman who sold scraps of things from door to door.

There was another woman from over the river who was very loud and unsophisticated, Vasiliki. I don't know what Mama used to see in her but she would speak to this woman and make her feel at home. She would sit and help with maybe the broad beans, or cutting vegetables for our dinner, and I would think, *all these people Mama? Why?*

There was always someone and perhaps I was a snob right from the beginning but I could not see why she had all of these people always around her. She just accepted everyone who came through the door, whether kings or paupers, she would take them in and speak to them, giving them any help they needed.

One of these women who lived further up in the middle of the village also befriended my mother. I only recall her surname 'Araouzena'. Not long after my little brother Thomas had died when Mama would have been quite vulnerable this woman really inserted herself into our lives. My mother was going about in a daze dressed in black, grieving for the loss of her second baby son. The village was steeped in superstition and witchcraft in those days and some of the village women considered themselves experts, becoming notorious for miles around. They tried to manipulate, and influence decisions taken by vulnerable people, especially with regard to arranged marriages and money deals. Although they may have claimed that exercising this influence was an act of kindness, it often seemed more inspired by malice.

It was such a woman who befriended my mother during the weeks following the death of Thomas. Sipping sweet black Cypriot coffee round the kitchen table they whispered for hours on end over the coming weeks. I was too young to comprehend the meaning of it all and I wasn't particularly interested as I was only about three years old. However, it all came to light one pleasant sunny day in late autumn. I was running about carefree at the back of the house near to some outbuildings trying to locate the eggs of the hens who roamed about. I was small and sturdy and full of life. I would climb walls and ladders and onto roofs looking for those eggs. I was one of those free spirited, carefree children, running about the fields and the gardens as I pleased. We had hen houses, pigs, animals everywhere and I loved to go and find where the hens laid their eggs and gather them up, still warm in my hands.

One day, Mama and this woman were right beside me as I ran about collecting the eggs. Usually I was left alone to do this, but on that morning, it was as if they were following me.

'Oh, you are looking the wrong way, Maro. You must really look in the right place for the eggs,' this woman said, with my mother standing beside her. 'I'll tell you where they are, shall I?'

I nodded. I could usually find them by myself but it couldn't hurt to get some help.

'They are in the oven!' she announced.

This oven, in the garden, was a dome like structure where a lot of baking of bread was done every week. It had a front with an opening and I didn't even question the silly idea that there would be eggs in there. I was very small and trusting when this happened, and certainly would have taken what she said as the truth.

'The eggs are in the oven!' she repeated, and Mama nodded beside her.

I was lifted up into the oven to find the eggs, but, of course, there were none. The oven looked very big to me as I clambered inside, crawling and searching, but I was quite sure I was looking in the wrong place.

'I cannot see any eggs,' I called. 'No eggs here.'

'Are you sure?' came one of their voices. I'm not sure which of them.

I was crawling around and around, and then I tried to get out. When I came to the opening of the oven, there was kindling in front of the mouth of the oven and the woman was standing there with my mother with matches in her hand. They were going to set it on fire.

'Let me out! Let me out!' I cried, but the fire suddenly started and I was terrified. I kept calling for them to let me out but no one helped.

'Are you going to stop eating your brothers?' the woman screamed at me.

I didn't know what she was talking about.

She said it three times. Eventually, I thought I might as well say 'yes' to get out of this situation! If I was silent or negative, I might be burned alive.

'Yes! I will stop eating them!' I agreed. 'I will stop eating my brothers!'

The kindling was put out and I was lifted from the oven. I don't know if it would have come to them burning me but they certainly wanted me to promise not to eat my brothers. I was so distressed that I ran away. I ran away as quickly as my little legs could carry me. My heart was thumping, I was so distressed. Frightened, I hid myself in the bushes at the far end of the garden for a very long time.

My father came home in the afternoon that day. Sometimes I would not see him until the evening, but this day he appeared. He was so annoyed with my mother, I heard him shouting at her, but I don't think he knew the whole story although her guilt at conspiring with that woman had made her confess some of it. He certainly had some idea. Mama showed a certain amount of regret to me, mostly about the fact that she had allowed herself to be persuaded by this ignorant and malicious woman. Many times over the years that followed my mother asked for forgiveness which I willingly gave, saying to her it was nothing, that I hardly remembered it but that wasn't true. I remembered it well and tears would come to my eyes each time, but I brushed it aside and carried on with whatever I was doing. In later years, during my visits to Cyprus, Mama would repeat the request of forgiveness each time and I would repeat my reply of it all being fine.

I'm not sure how badly I was affected by it – as an adult, I studied psychology and learned a great deal about the developmental years and the effect on one's future life. That has led me to believe that I don't think I've ever resolved that episode. It seems as if it is destined to live with me forever, it is part of me now and really – why would it not be? It is quite horrific.

A lot happened around that time of my life and, on reflection, I can see that my mother was quite contradictory – she was pragmatic but religious, generous to others but not warm to me, kind but she thrashed me. I believe she had been disciplined a lot during her own upbringing, that was how she was brought up and she just thought that was how it was with your children. Maybe I was a naughty child but, many a time, she would chase me, running around the field, shouting for me, ready to hit me when she finally caught me up. She was the same with Chrysoula but not with my younger siblings who would come in later years. People, however, do change.

I wasn't close to my father really, he was always away, he worked and worked and worked. He would come home late at night and be too tired to talk on many occasions. Papa was strict but I can't remember him hitting me, unlike my mother. She certainly did most of the physical punishment but he was very authoritative, his tone of voice would keep you in line quite easily. I suppose I was a little frightened of him. If he asked me to do anything, I would do it without hesitation. As a result, that brought a certain amount of positivity to our relationship but only in that I did what he wanted, cleaning the irrigation stream, or watering the newly planted peppers. Even as a very small child he would say to me, 'That is how I want you to do it.' and that is how it would be done.

The climate made irrigation channels necessary and inevitably they would get silted up with stones and leaves, especially after the winter and it was assumed that I would clear them correctly, even when I was such a little thing. Papa knew that I would and gave me a lot of responsibility, pretty much from as soon as I could walk.

Sometimes at the table he would talk about his work at the car rental business, if he wasn't too weary, perhaps someone had hired a car and had an accident. He would be worried about insurance and all the aspects of his job, but if we giggled as he spoke, there would be consequences – sometimes he would make me leave the room without any food. However, he was not violent towards me, it was left to Mama to do all of the real discipline. I cannot really say whether the incident with the oven made me more wary of her, whether I thought there might be a repeat of the situation, but I can certainly say that it never left me.

I helped my mother a lot in sweeping the yards of leaves, they could not be left dirty. She would give me the broom and I worked well. When she told me that abroad there were brooms who worked for themselves, I was amazed! She meant a vacuum of course but I just couldn't picture it. How could a machine do such things? I still remember my astonishment when she told me.

I don't think I was close to Mama as a child. I accepted my relationship with her and thought it was normal. There were quite a lot of us and she was a very busy woman, and probably, in retrospect, we were brought up by the scruff of the neck. We brought ourselves up really. It was more like a teacher and pupil relationship when I think of it. She was there to guide us and look after our physical needs but that was all. I accepted her being there but not as a provider of cuddles or love or warmth. She gave me the practical things but not the emotional. She did give me that responsibility from a very young age but I was a capable child anyway, independent and aware of my life as a working child.

There was much to be done, and I wasn't going to be indulged or treated like a little princess. I was forever working in the fields, gathering almonds or olives, lemons or bananas, anything really because we had everything at our fingertips. I helped with the crops from as early in my life as I could. We had some seasonal workers but only when they were really needed, maybe once a year. In between times, it was us. If there was a good fall of, say, olives, under the trees in autumn at the end of August, Mama would say, 'Come on Maro, let's go. We have work to do.' She wouldn't ask my sister, it was always me.

Chrysoula had the excuse of not being very robust, she was a very thin girl, but it was mostly because she was unwilling that she didn't work like me. It was not easy to persuade her to do anything if she was disinclined. I was a very helpful child, I was into hard work from the beginning whereas my sister would say, 'No, I won't do it.' She would fall out with my father, and although she wasn't a very strong child, she didn't eat much, she was just determined not to do things and I think that was the real reason for her stubbornness. Contrary to her, I would eat my food and want more, which was, of course, the reason I was a little chubby. She would only eat half a potato, I would eat everything I could see. We were such different personalities and I was definitely a favourite with my father. Unfortunately, my sister was very much aware of that, and she resented me because of it.

Chapter Four

Chrysoula was two years older than I. We had very different personalities – she was fiery, insisting on her own way. I was determined too but in a quieter, more calculated way. She was very like my father and I was like Mama. Like him, she had the gift of the gab. I did not, I even had a lisp. I would get frustrated and much to my regret I would resort to making references to her slightly, impaired right arm as I knew that would hurt her.

During her breach birth, the local doctor was called to assist the midwife. Instead of placing his instruments on either side of her head, he grabbed the top of her arm, damaging the nerve to the muscle. When Chrysoula was young she was aware of the defect and would subconsciously try to hide it by having it hanging slightly forwards and inwards. Our parents did everything they could to deal with the problem. She was taken to the best paediatrician in Nicosia, where exercise was recommended but unfortunately there were no physiotherapists around at the time. They did however employ a physical education teacher from the gymnasium (school) but to no avail.

Mama and Papa made things worse by always making remarks about Chrysoula's arm, asking her to make some effort, to put her arm in the right place and walk straight. Although we had our differences, those ongoing remarks upset me terribly, in fact they probably planted the first seeds for my future career as a physiotherapist.

Compared to my sister Chrysoula, I was always 'piggy will' and she was 'piggy will not'. I was willing to work and always open to being given responsibilities. I was the one who would run about, happy in the garden and because I was an able, strong and determined child, my father always used to give me tasks – to water the bushes that had just been planted, or the crops, or clean the irrigation channel. I would do it willingly whereas Chrysoula would simply say she did not want to. At the end of the day, Father would pay me for my work. I had a piggy bank for it, the same piggy bank I had hoped to fill with an extra pound when Father had offered me that sum to touch the silkworms. I would sit in front of the fire on cold pre-school winter days, using a knife to get all of my shillings and pennies out of the little bank so that I could count them. I just liked to have that knowledge of being secure.

Despite their romantic beginnings and their fight to be together, my parents didn't really show love to each other. I think their relationship was more about companionship. In those days, you didn't go about showing affection as a couple, there was no constant cuddling or kissing as the next generation developed, especially in the UK. I never saw them hugging or giving a kiss to each other. Poor Mama – her married life was not a bed of roses. She never complained but I was an observant child and perhaps knew what was happening around me more than my siblings. Latterly, in my adult life, she confided in me and mentioned one or two episodes which confirmed my suspicions that Father was not faithful to her.

He was not a loving family man. In common with many men at that time, he saw his role as a husband and father as providing for the material needs of his family. I must have only been a few years old when I found Mama sitting at the table silently crying. I reached up to her but I was certainly too young to know the right questions to ask. She was distressed when somebody from the village told her that my father had been seen near our Carob estate by the hill, walking hand in hand with an English lady during his working day. It was reputed to be Lady French who would be in our lives for many years to come – was he indeed having an affair with her? Every morning he would take with him a bunch of freshly cut flowers from the garden, whatever happened to be in season at the time. It was one of my jobs, along with Chrysoula, to cut these flowers so that he could take them with him to someone.

One thing I can remember is that, when I was little, Mother and Father would sometimes go a place by the sea called Zephyros. This was an open-air nightclub up on the cliffs overlooking the bay. Behind it was the mountain of Pentadactylos. It was floodlit and one could see the colourful lights for miles around. There would be a band playing too. It was a lovely place where people were happy, dancing and eating good food. I had a good time there. I would be given a mezze, a platter of little appetisers, alongside everyone sitting around the side of the dance floor. We were allowed to taste wine from a very young age and Zephyros was known for serving delightful wines and cognac. At maybe three or four years of age, you would get a spot of wine and water to try. It was a very different culture to that of northern Europe, withthe culture of binge drinking. Mama and Papa would dance together at Zephyros and I do remember them enjoying each other's company on those nights. I would get tired after a little while - especially with a bit of wine! – and I'd go down the steps away from all the music and onto a deckchair overlooking the sea across to the West where I would doze off. I could hear the music drifting through, it was all so pleasant. I would get woken up to walk back to the car. I was never carried as that would be an indulgence, and it would all be so nice. Those are the only memories I have of them being affectionate with each other.

Papa still felt bound to his siblings and mother, he was very much the successful one and he carried that responsibility all of his life. He tried to settle his sister Irene by arranging her marriage with the man she was engaged to. He bought her a house, with some land and provided for her. He also gave money to his mother every week when he saw her. He had a sense of duty, that is for certain. My aunt decided she did not want this man after all as she did not really love him, and she wanted to go off with another fellow called Christos. Christos was working on a nearby farm with sheep and goats, but he had a family of four children already. He was a man of medium height, very solid-looking, with piercing blue eyes. I remember that he was rather coarse, but love does not make distinctions – Irene loved him and she wanted him, so they lived together, which was regarded as being quite shocking in those days. She was very like my father, determined and stubborn, characteristics which pervaded his family and mine y for many years to come. My father was absolutely furious that Irene had fallen for Christos and he argued vociferously with her, he did not even want her in our house, which was ironic given that he and Mama had faced so many similar barriers to their love.

Christos and Irene worked hard on their smallholding of a few acres and became subsistence farmers. They built a little reservoir, acquired a few sheep, made halloumi cheese, had goats, hens, pigs, and were very happy. They even had a Turk from the village to help them out which was very unusual. Father would be at work during the day and, without his knowledge, Mama would take us to Lapithos to visit them. They were always pleased to see us and extremely hospitable. They would lay the table for a meal in the backyard surrounded by jasmine bushes and flowers and protected above by the overhanging vine, the aroma of the jasmine bush and lemon groves pervading the air. The house was very clean and tidy, Aunt Irene looked after it well. All the yards were spotless and she had a big table under the vine trees, which would be set in no time, ready for the magnificent spread of food which was presented effortlessly and speedily in such a beautiful setting. She was always welcoming, feeding us, invariably killing a chicken there and then for us; she was a sweet woman. Irene had a temper, like my father, but she was good to us. Papa knew nothing of our visits. He never forgave her, they never made up and we never visited with him.

Irene was talkative and interested in all of us, she was quite similar to my father in some ways but obviously they followed different life education and experiences. We were always instructed to keep quiet about our visits to her. Sometimes Auntie Irene would visit us in Karavas but if she heard her brother's car coming along the long drive, she would quickly leave through the back door.

Papa's other sibling, Uncle Nicholas, was different in looks and personality. He was very laidback, not determined in his nature at all, which would make sense if he indeed did have a different father. The only time I remember him being around was when he stayed with us a short time before emigrating. He was a quiet man, especially in my father's presence. My parents tried to make all the settled preparations for his journey to London, as well as giving him plenty of advice. He established himself as a barber in Walthamstow but never kept in touch and his relationship with the rest of the siblings fizzled out.

I used to hear these stories while women talked the way they do, I listened to it all, absorbed it all. There was a strong community of women in our village, and I am sure, in every village like ours. The hospital was in Kyrenia, eight miles away which, in those days, was too far away if you had no access to transport. This meant that there was a reliance on wise women if they could help and village midwives who would help women to give birth, only getting a doctor if absolutely necessary. All of the women knew each other, they probably knew who had brought them into life. I certainly did. It was a connection between women and they would help each other out whenever they could – and they would also gossip a great deal, which is when I would listen and add to my knowledge.

Father's mother was a peasant and she would talk about everything that had happened with him, about how she had initiated their marriage, about how she was the one who manipulated it all from the night of the storm onwards. Once we all were born and mother was settled into the house, Grandmother Eleni would still come and often bring delicious figs from her tree. Mother would give her food but was unsophisticated. Although Mother claimed that she did not want us to look down on Eleni, I felt that she did. As a child you pick up on that.

Quite often my grandmother would go upstairs and go to sleep on the veranda after lunch. I would follow but she said very little. By that time, she was starting to suffer from bowel cancer and died at the age of 55, and I think she was an unwell woman on those times when she disappeared upstairs. I remember her just lying there, saying nothing to me. When she died, I thought she was so old and therefore had no wish to live beyond that age. I've since changed my mind! No children were allowed to go to the funeral which was the custom at the time.

Customs and rites were a very important part of life in Karavas, and, naturally, Church was very important to our way of life as a family who lived in the Greek Orthodox tradition. There was a main church in the middle of the village but there were others too. Saint Irene for example, was up in the foothills of the mountain. The one in the middle of the village, was called St Evangelistria, a relatively modern, larger church but the little one up on the hill was very picturesque, small, white, and very old nestling into the side of the hill. Most of the time, especially during the winter, we would to go to the nearby Church of St Evangelistria, the weather being bad, but in spring we would go up the hill into Saint Irene.

Religion gave us structure and we regularly attended the Sunday service. Mother liked Sunday school for us. It mattered to her and it was the central point of our Sundays, which were very structured and predictable. Church was also a community, an extension of the life we had in the village. My father only went to church at Christmas, Easter and during the baptism of my siblings. He was not brought up in religion. My mother, on the other hand, was steeped in religion. My maternal grandfather was a man of the Church – not so my grandmother. She was a free spirit in every way, not a conformist, a real eccentric I would say.

At Easter time we would go to church early in the morning. The whole yard and Church, after the 'Good Word' (Christ is risen), are flooded with candles and extreme care is taken to transport the candlelight home as this is regarded a good omen for the family. Once home a big feast follows, parties take place in order to make up for the fasting of the last few weeks prior to Easter. Everyone would shake hands, say *Christ is Risen!* to each other and light candles, with a big bonfire blazing in the church yard (burning Judas Iscariot).

I would only have been about three years old, but I still remember my excitement when Mama announced there would be an overnight vigil in the church of Acheropoietos. The prospect of staying awake all night was wonderful. There had been a drought for a long period of time and all the people came that night to pray to St Mary. The Church was packed full and over spilling. Mother was sitting on the steps over at the left-hand side of the church and I was beside her. An hour or two into the service, I became uneasy, very tired and unhappy. I really wanted my bed; I climbed onto Mama's knee and fell fast asleep.

Acheropoietos Monastery was situated high up on the rocks by the sea. Acheropoietos relates to the ancient icon of Saint Mary and it means the icon made without hands. Many years ago, there used to be a thriving community of monks but during my early years, most of the monks' cells were empty with only the occasional eccentric British visitor staying in the West Wing. I remember my father visiting a Scotsman who was staying there, probably a recluse. The priest quite often would stay in the monastery too and sometimes I could see a brown Labrador dog with a small, closed tin container hanging round its neck, steadily walking along the path through my grandmother's olive grove heading for the monastery to deliver the lunch entrusted to him by the priest's wife (Papathia) to give the priest.

The church of Acheropoitos was dark and gloomy with many pillars and arches. My maternal grandfather (my pappous), who was an eminent figure within the community and a headmaster in one of the nearby villages, would often participate in the sermon and he always, always, wanted to sing. Although his singing voice was not good, he would sing solo in the church, and no one would stop him because of his status. When I was a little older, and the service was going on and on and on, I would escape with some of my friends through the side door, go down the many steps and onto the pebbly beach. The sea was turquoise, clean and inviting. We would chase each other, gather shells and compete in throwing stones into the sea, having such fun-filled days. There was fresh, crystal-clear water coming out of the spring carved out through the ages and trickling down into a pool below. The spring was known as 'Pappous', the grandfather, as it was so ancient. This was a popular and noisy gathering place after the service came to an end on Sundays. It was certainly a great deal more fun than listening to the droning in the church.

During the week, when there was no one about, the beach was heavenly. The only sound to be heard was the murmur of the sea and the trickling water of the spring. I have memories of this beach ever since I can remember. I learned to swim breaststroke here. Father taught me when I was very young despite the sharp stones cutting into my tender little feet. Further on the left the bay was treacherous. There was a whirlpool which had taken lives of many people, including a young boy of only ten years. His parents were poor, he was their only child and lived further up the village at the foot of the mountain. The whole village mourned.

In Church, the men and women sat separately as was the tradition at that time. Even at school, the boys and girls would be on separate sides, both in the classroom and playground. It was all about upholding standards and imposing ideas of what was 'right', even if those ideas seem ridiculous to us now.

These are all such beautiful memories to me. I know that what was instilled in me during those early years of my life helped me transform into the woman I am. My early life laid the foundation that enabled me to be strong and fight for what I needed, and sometimes just what I wanted. When you are not indulged, when you are encouraged to work, almost from the moment you can walk, there is value to that. When you are given, indeed when you seek, responsibility, there is a value to that too. It provides a resolve within you which can be drawn on in later times when the world provides you with many challenges. I lived in a wonderful place where I was secure and welcomed by everyone who lived in the village, the happy child who was always reliable, but who had such spirit – the little girl who was showing already the type of woman she would become.

Sir Arthur, who had been my Papa's rescuer, saviour and employer, died when I was only about five years old. He became very unwell and died extremely quickly after his illness took over. I wasn't privy to any of that, or to his condition. The family story is Sir Arthur decreed that if Papa attended his funeral, he would be beneficiary to his car and also, I suspect, a substantial sum of money. A car was a big gift to be given as there were very few about in those days and father was delighted. The main thing he did with this bequest was to start a car rental and taxi business. This was the beginning of my father's various businesses. He was also pleased with the money with which he bought property and invested in young lemon trees which later became a lucrative business.

I sensed that father was sad when Sir Arthur died as he had been like a father to him but I wonder why would he have made the condition of his will dependent on Papa going to the funeral? I would have thought he would have done so anyway. I do remember visiting him with my parents and Chrysoula but sadly I do not recall him personally. The only thing I remember was the big fish tank on the left-hand side of the long corridor hanging on the wall of his house, on the outskirts of Kyrenia. Chrysoula was able to have a good look while I was left standing underneath it. I obviously made a great deal of fuss and I was lifted up by Mama to see the fish – I was fascinated but I do not remember meeting Sir Arthur.

The consequences of the bequest would affect all of my life to come. I was still naïve, still so young – and I had no idea that darker days would arrive as an indirect impact of what had been given to Papa and his relationship with his benefactor.

Acheropoietos monastery

Chapter Five

Mama valued education so much as she was trained as a teacher herself – in those days, to be a teacher in our village was an important thing and very rare for a woman. Of course, you had to have the brains and ability, but if you were a woman, you also needed the ability to fight against what was expected of you and to know your own worth – especially if you were a mother too. She did not work as a teacher when I was very little, although that would come later, and I feel that must have been frustrating for her even if she did see her main role as that of a mother.

Women were not thought of in the same way in those days. In the very rare event that they had any academic credentials or any desire to have a career, it was all expected to fall by the wayside for them to become wives and mothers. Those were their 'natural' roles and it was seen as somewhat inappropriate if they veered away from them. Mama was trained as a primary school teacher and was very good at maths. She was always looking for new ways to teach it and always to teach others, but her opportunities to be a teacher herself were very limited when we were babies. However, her love of maths showed itself in other ways. She was very practical and very good at solving problems. She was a pragmatic woman.

A lot of this came from how she was raised as her own father was a clever man, a headmaster with scholarships from his birthplace of Syros, the capital island of the Cyclades.

Pappous valued education too and it was an environment which coloured my childhood. Education mattered and so did external validation.

The relationship of a parent with their child so many years ago was completely different from the one we have now. I don't remember always being cuddled and kissed, constantly being told how wonderful I was, or being treated like a little princess. In Britain especially, parents take their child and make them feel they are the most important thing in the world – while that may seem nice it can prevent them from developing independence and resilience. Things which will stand them in better stead than being told every single thing they do is remarkable, no matter how insignificant it is. Children should know that they are the centre of their parents' world but not the centre of the world itself. I think Mama was generally a good mother if not a warm one – she allowed us to bring ourselves up, and that is a gift in a way, which brought benefits in later life.

She had so many children, but she had also lost so many and those losses must have taken a toll. She was in charge of a lot of land with a lot of produce, she worked hard to manage all of that, looking after workers and making sure everything ran smoothly. My father just concentrated on his business while Mama carried everything else.

Mama had been raised the middle of three, with an elder sister (who was also a teacher), and a younger brother who was the centre of the world for their family. To have a son in those days was the ultimate prize, and nothing a girl could do would ever be enough compared to what a boy would achieve. Her brother was sent to Athens for years, not only to obtain a degree in dentistry but also one in medicine as a 'double degree' was the norm back then. The fact that he was called 'Dr' at the end of his studies was considered the most wonderful thing. For my grandparents, not only had they been blessed with a son after two daughters, but the son was a doctor – it was very high status. However, on that side of my family, it seemed to me that women held the key to many things.

My maternal grandmother, Despina Shilantoni, was a very tough woman with an extremely strong personality and very wealthy. While my Pappous was recognised as someone with education and brains, a clever man from the Cyclades, she was very wealthy in her own right. Unusually for that time, her property didn't go to him when they married, and she maintained all of the land which was in her possession. It was the way in those days that everything would be handed to the man when the couple wed, but she simply wouldn't do it. When she wed Nicholas Kalava, an emigrant from Syros she married into a family who had been bakers on the island. Nicholas was one of six children, with four brothers and two sisters. One of the brothers made his home in Athens whilst the rest of the siblings settled in Cyprus, together with their parents. Nicholas was an intelligent boy at an early age and was spotted by a bishop who proceeded to educate him. Eventually he became a teacher, a respected profession in those days and very soon he became a headmaster but Despina and Nicholas were completely different in education, culture, attitudes and beliefs.

The marriage of my grandparents was not made in heaven. Many arranged marriages in those days were not good matches, the backgrounds were totally different and there was no real affection. Like most women of her generation, my grandmother was not educated despite the fact that her family was wealthy. My grandmother was an early suffragette in my mind by refusing to hand over her property on marriage to her husband, despite the law of the land in those days. She was strong-minded and very stubborn, in charge of her property and wealth until her dying days.

In Britain, a woman of her means would have staff to attend to her every need, she would sit back and do nothing, but, no, that was not how Stete lived her life. She owned so much land and she worked it with her bare hands every day of her life alongside her workers. She also had another way of earning money. People would come to her for a loan which she would grant, with interest, from her own money.

Her position and her wealth came from her family who had owned land for a long time. She was born in the late 1800s of Venetian origin according to our uncle who traced the family tree. The Venetians had been in Cyprus for many hundreds of years before the Turks took over for another 300 years, and when the Turks were in charge, they allowed the family to keep their estate – I think this was probably because they were in the suburbs and were seen as less important. The family had their own crest which can be seen to this day up in the North of one of the villages near Lapithos, engraved in stone near the watermill. Stete's people were the owners of the mill which was used for grinding grain in the area. The water from the spring was used to irrigate the land for miles around.

Her family had a lot of status and they kept that status even when the Turks took over. Throughout history, Cyprus had been attacked. The Venetians occupied Cyprus in 1489, when the independent Kingdom of Cyprus ended. The strategic position of Cyprus made it desirable to many invaders, amongst them the Ottoman Empire in 1571 and the British Empire in 1878. For the Venetians, Cyprus was important commercially but it was primarily a military base. Greek Cypriots throughout the ages had been forced to find ways to survive – they are hardworking and resilient people to this day.

Stete was happiest when working in the fields, she wasn't typical of her class or of her times. She must also have valued education a great deal – a couple of years before my mother died, she told me, as a young girl, in order for her to continue with her further education at the Gymnasium, she was taken to Nicosia on the back of a donkey for twenty miles over the mountains to attend the Academy, given that there were no buses or other transport. My grandmother had been the one to ensure that happened.

Stete was not an easy kind of woman, she was at odds with everybody, I remember that. She was not a compliant woman, she stood for what she believed and I would see a lot of that as I followed her about a great deal. I was a child who loved to be outside, and because she worked on the land constantly, it made sense for me to be with her. I admired Stete's determination, but she did come across as eccentric. Her character was one of pragmatism and of doing things her way; she would argue if she had to and would always stand up for her rights – or what she believed those rights to be. She certainly never dressed as a woman of money and would often be seen in the jackets that came down from the men of the family. She had goats who lived in a large stable in a little clearing and sometimes she would even sleep with them if they were having kids or if they were sick.

I didn't want to be like her but I did enjoy the time we spent together. There were times when she would say, 'Let's have some lunch, Maro.' However, she would completely ignore my mother who might only be a few hundred yards away. Instead, she would take me by the hand and decide to build a fire right where we were standing so that she could cook some food. There were often utensils stacked up at the side of the little clearing - I guess because this was something she did so often - and she would place a big frying pan on top of a makeshift fire, cutting lots of fresh peppers, onions, aubergines, everything that was growing nearby, and that would be our lunch. It was delicious. She certainly had no airs or graces and would sit there on the ground, eating from her hands like anyone else in the fields would do. She was a very basic woman with no need for frills or frivolity, and, as a child, I appreciated that. What little one wouldn't enjoy the idea of a spontaneous picnic? I never found it odd that she wouldn't call my mother over when she was so nearby, I just enjoyed the moment for what it was, which was how Stete lived too.

I was a very wild sort of child and there is no doubt that sometimes I would go over the top and really annoy my mother. I would push her so far that she would thrash me. There is one occasion which I remember very well. My sister Chrysoula and I never really got on together as children, we had very different natures and personalities. As she was a couple of years older than me, she generally got things first. One day, Mother bought some brand-new material for Chrysoula's new uniform. I was not to get one. I was very jealous and also furious at what I saw as an injustice. I went off to the kitchen, got some scissors, and snipped a tiny little bit off the end of the cloth. Mama reacted with such anger, storming off to get a leather belt, and thrashing me quite severely.

When these things happened, I would go to Stete who I would invariably find in her little clearing in the big field above the family house. This was eventually inherited by my uncle. We wouldn't speak of what happened but she would know I had been beaten. My mother was not close to her which meant there would be no clash of loyalties – in fact, the only child Stete cared about was her son. Anything she had was given to him. Everyone knew that she favoured him above all else; it was just accepted in the same way as when my brother Andreas was born, I just lived with the fact that he was the priority. That seems like a very stoic statement but it ran through the generations and I had seen it with Stete and her children, which meant that I knew what would happen. The sons became little emperors and everyone accepted and absorbed it. I didn't mind Andreas getting all of the attention, he was often carried about as if he was a prince on a throne, but I knew that was just the way, and I guess my mother knew it too – she'd lived it as a sister and she encouraged it when she had a son.

I was four when my long-awaited brother Andreas was born, thankfully perfect, a beautiful child with lots of blonde curls. My father was over the moon at the birth of his third son after the death of two boys. He only had eyes for Andreas who was taken with him everywhere, carried over his shoulder and adored. Mother was delighted too of course, finally they had a boy. I wasn't particularly jealous or upset over the arrival of my baby brother on the scene, I just watched with interest as mother played with him in his cot and looked after him. I was also very much pre-occupied with the nature around me, playing with the fluffy newly born chicks, and the kittens. They were much more interesting than a baby. I played outside a great deal in the gardens, eating almonds and fruit, everything was so plentiful. I also played with the neighbourhood children particularly a boy called Stavros. His mother was a great friend of Mama and she often visited. Unfortunately, she suffered from schizophrenia in her thirties and relationships changed and became rather difficult.

Another memory comes to mind. When I was about four, my mother asked me one lunchtime to get a marrow from my grandmother's field going down to the sea. She had tomatoes, peanuts and cucumbers growing there too. On my way back, by the time I got to the olive grove, the thunder and lightning was terrible, with a downpour which made me think I would drown there and then. I was so frightened of the thunder and lightning walking back to the house, but that shows how much freedom I have. It happened again when I was six; I remember another downpour, an absolute flood. When something like that happened, you could not run from A to B, you had to stop and wait. I was at school by then and had finished for the day. It was about 1pm (we started very early), and we were all to be held back, but I was fearless and decided to go. By the time I reached my uncle's house, I was completely soaked. I went in the basement – only 500 yards from school – then began running through the olive groves up to my house. Finally, I got home to a fire burning in the kitchen and a big pot of lentil soup (flat lentils were my favourite). We were all round the fire, my grandfather too, and that is a good memory, all of us together.

We had a big cage full of rabbits, some for eating but not the black or white ones, just the grey ones – I don't know why. Mother would lift them by the neck and twist them to kill them. I liked the rabbits especially when they were little, and the killing of them turned three of my siblings vegan. We also had rows of beehives at the end of our rose garden, past the asparagus field. It was a great day when the beekeeper came, dressed in his special suit with a big brimmed hat and veil. I loved the honeycomb. We had everything; we were completely self-sufficient.

We had no electricity at that point. Although we were prosperous and had much more than most in the area, everything was basic and quite primitive compared to northern Europe and the UK. For many years, the toilet was at the end of the garden. Every night before bed, we had to go for a visit to this dome like building which I was very scared of, I thought I would land in the slit in the middle. I wasn't afraid of much, but during the winter, you could hear the sea moaning. I would say in the night, 'What is that noise, Mama?' She would answer, 'It is just the waves, Maro, just the waves.'

Right from the beginning, I wanted to lead in whatever way I could. I liked the idea of being in charge. Was it a personality trait? I believe so. I would have hated to be a follower. Within a big family, everyone needs to find their place. As the second born, perhaps my need to be in front was always scuppered by not being the first child, but it was something I could try to achieve in other ways. Chrysoula was competitive too but we were such different personalities. She flared up so quickly, but I would sit back and think about things. I wouldn't say I was easy-going as I always wanted to strive and achieve, but I was never an angry person. Mother did have a confident air as of course did my father as he dealt with so many people of status. We are all a combination of nature and nurture and it was certainly very obvious in me. My family was full of ambitious people so there may be a genetic element but also I observed their drive to achieve what was important to them. To my father, this was to be a success in business; to Irene to live a happy family life with the man she loved and with Stete to be beholden to no-one.

On reflection, I can see that my character showed itself from a very early age – and nowhere does it show itself more clearly than in what I think of as 'the incident of the earrings.'

The relationship between godchild and godparent is important in Cyprus. I was always rather confused as to who my godmother was – there were two women, a mother and daughter, and the younger one, Irene, was a friend of my mother. These women lived together (along with Gregoris,

Irene's husband) and shared the household duties so I was always confused as a child as to whether my godmother was the young one (which as a child I would have preferred), or the old one. I now think that maybe they shared godmother duties too.

The first stage of the child's christening is the religious ceremony with the priest, then after a few days there is a ceremony with the clothes the child wore. The long silk gown, the little cap on their head, and any other things, are placed in a towel to be washed after three days. This responsibility falls to the nonos or nona, the godfather or godmother, and it is seen as very important. I believe that it was at the point of the christening that the confusion over who was my godmother arose. It was meant to be the younger one, Irene, but she was menstruating at the time when the washing rites of the baby's clothes were due so, at this point, Maritsou (the mother) had to take over. It would have been considered unclean for Irene to wash the christening clothes so she carried me into the church and held me during the service but was not to conduct these other duties. Her mother did the cleansing rites and therefore acquired certain 'rights' over me.

It was a very outmoded way of thinking, but if a woman was bleeding, she was kept from holy communion – an excuse I made the most of when I got older although I did miss the sweet wine on those occasions! Although the older woman got some of the responsibilities of a godmother, it was always the younger one who would give me gifts. Irene would come to me on my birthday with gold bangles, or at other times bring cloth to make me a dress, perhaps buy me my first shoes. These were all the duties of the nona.

I loved the gold bangles I was given but I was desperate for earrings and absolutely delighted when Irene brought me a pair. They were gold, tiny, the shape of a heart with a ruby in the middle. Such perfect little things. There was only one problem – I didn't have pierced ears as I was too young.

'I will put these away safely for you, Maro,' said my mother. 'When you are older, then you can get your ears pierced and they will be waiting for you until then. You are far too young.'

I suppose she was right given that I wasn't even at school yet, but I was very upset. A few days later, on one hot lunchtime, Mama was having her siesta and I couldn't stop thinking about those beautiful earrings. I knew where she had hidden them, so carefully I crept to her room, retrieved them while she still slept and planned the next stage of my adventure. All I needed to do was get my ears pierced – how hard could that be?

I knew who could help me and I was determined, and I had no doubt in my mind that I would get what I wanted. With the earrings in my hand, I trotted off down the road to the house of the local GP. Apprehensively, I knocked on the door (the doorknob was far too high for me) and the wife of the doctor opened. She was just who I wanted.

'I would like my ears pierced please,' I told her, boldly. I don't know why I thought she would do it, maybe she had a reputation for it and I suppose she would have access to needles.

She looked at me as if I had asked for the most natural thing in the world, then took me through the door on the left of the house so that I could wait for her to get everything together that she would need. The house was absolutely quiet, you could hear a pin drop. Her husband, the doctor, must have been having his siesta. She took such a long time that I started to worry – she did come back eventually and did the piercing quickly, silently and efficiently. She just pushed a needle through each lobe and then placed some threads in so that they wouldn't close over and sent me on my way. Can you imagine? A little tiny girl just going to someone's house alone and asking for that, and for it to be done?

I skipped home with my ears pierced and all I can remember was that I wasn't told off, although mother was clearly surprised. Luckily, I didn't get an infection and after a few days I could wear my little golden hearts with the ruby in the centre. They were such lovely earrings which I cherished for many years until one was lost in later life, which upset me a great deal.

The 'incident of the earrings' says so much about me I feel. My determination and belief that, of course, if I wanted something, why should it not happen? As my life progressed, such determination would remain, but I would discover just how much hard work there needed to be to ensure that my beliefs and wants would always come to fruition.

Chapter Six

You cannot live where I lived without the past being a character in your story. Myths and legends were all around me, from the stories we were told and learned at school, to the people we knew. Some of those people lived or acted in a way which may seem alien to people now, but there was a strong sense of superstition and power running through my life in Cyprus and it seemed perfectly acceptable. My maternal grandmother was very superstitious. I picked up many ideas of what may or may not cause good or bad luck from her, and my mother continued that as did most of the women in our family.

If you are doing well and you present yourself in a very superior way to others, they envy you and there was a way to protect yourself from that. Even now if you go to Greece, you can buy necklaces and brooches to avert the evil eye. We had lots of those tokens as Mother believed in them completely. She liked us to adhere to tradition, such as on May 1st, we would be encouraged to go out and get some dew from the grass, put it on our faces and pray to become beautiful. She probably wasn't as superstitious as some but she was brought up with it and couldn't break free however educated she was. It's hard to shake off how you were raised. I didn't always wear the necklace, I just chose to do so sometimes. I always chose what I wanted whenever I could – I was that sort of child.

We didn't get electricity or appliances like washing machines at home until I was about ten years old, which meant that household duties were very time-consuming and, of course, all of that fell to women. Washing day was on a Monday and followed very precise procedures which Mama undertook with someone she hired to help. After the actual washing itself had been done, mostly in an area outside, the garments were taken to a special area which I would describe as a large slab. This was very big, a very strong slab of rock where the washing was beaten with something which looked rather like a tennis racquet, washed and rinsed then it would be left to dry in the sun. One day, I had been out with Mama and Chrysoula while the washing dried. It was late afternoon by the time we returned and we all went to bring the washing indoors. There on the rock slab was the strangest thing. There was a pile of little dolls, tiny figures like voodoo dolls, lying there. They had obviously been placed there deliberately and they didn't belong to us, so there had to be some sort of purpose – a magical purpose I believe.

'What are they for?' I asked my mother. 'What is the meaning of them?'

She seemed a little upset and angry, scooping them up and throwing them in the bin. 'This is to do with your uncle,' she said, angrily. 'I know it. This is to do with someone in the village who thinks that they can cast a love spell. These *things* are to make him fall in love and marry someone – I don't know who, but I will not have it, I will not have these love spells.'

Uncle Panayiotis was a very desirable bachelor. Mama was very angry about this but she wasn't a person who would really dwell on things or allow something like that to upset her for long. However, it stuck in my mind as that was the environment we lived in, with people in the village who believed in such superstitions. No matter how clever Mother was, she was still affected and could never really shake off the superstitions which surrounded her.

Even when women did nothing more outlandish than live alone, the village labelled them as witches. My paternal grandmother had a cousin who lived up on the hills by herself in a little cottage near the foothills of the mountains. On her own, with cats, she was the subject of much discussion, When I was a child, I could hear everyone talking about her but there was nothing unusual other than she had chosen to live there on her own terms. Even when she adopted a little girl, probably to look after her in her old age, she was looked upon with fear and suspicion. Alone and with cats *and* a woman? Well, that must make her a witch!

There were a few other women in the village who did not fall into the categories of wives or mothers which made them the subject of gossip too. People made up such things about them, such as one woman being seen with lit candles in a crown on her head walking towards an area that was supposed to be haunted. Women were meant to fit into certain roles – those who didn't? Well, it was easier to label them witches than to actually look at whether women could be anything which was a little different.

The villagers would intertwine stories about places too, which made it hard to separate fact from fiction. There was a particular river called Vathirkakas (deep river), with terrible drops down to the bottom, running at the side of one of our fields in Lapithos. There were beautiful anemones, cyclamens and wildflowers covering the entire area and, in spring, I would go there with Chrysoula, to gather armfuls of them. We had to be brave, it felt like a real adventure, as we had heard such stories of the place. There were so many tales of ghosts walking along the river's edge, beating drums and making the terrible music of the dead. As children do, we would work ourselves up into a fright, terrifying each other by talking about the stories that we had heard. We would never have ventured into the river itself, or even the embankment, for fear that we would never escape, no doubt being pulled down into the underworld by the spirits who walked the land, looking for souls such as ours. There were such beautiful cyclamens on the embankment and I really wanted them so badly but was also terrified. Of course, looking back, I can see that these stories would be kept alive by the adults to try and keep us from danger, but for me, it was just another terror to face.

There were so many things which gave people comfort or made them worry about what was going to happen – whatever emotion or fear you felt, there would be a sign to fit.

If a couple got married, on their wedding night, they would take a male child and roll him on the double bed to encourage the conception of a boy!

If you heard an owl hooting near the house, that was a bad omen and someone would be likely to die.

The first person you encounter in the morning, well, your day will go according to who you have seen – they will influence your day completely. The worst scenario would be to see a priest. If you saw one of them with their hat, big black beard and long coat, you would have a very bad day indeed.

You would put a ribbon from a wedding under your pillow to dream of your future husband.

A woman after having a child, had to be confined to the house for forty days in order for the woman to return back to her former mental and physical self. After those forty days, she would have to visit the priest in order to be cleansed before she could enter normal life again. I suppose that is also linked to menstruating women not being allowed into Church.

People were very much affected by dreams and would try to translate them into some meaning. If you saw a barking dog, that would mean you had an enemy. A snake would signify someone who really hated you and was lurking, ready to attack.

If you go to bed and your wardrobe is open, you must close it otherwise spirits would come out in the middle of the night.

Although educated and scornful of old wives' tales, Mother would take holy water from Church and sprinkle it into every corner of the house to ward off evil spirits. She was a very good reader of the Greek coffee dregs and became an expert over the years, with friends and family coming to her to see what she could predict. This was something which people believed in deeply and absolutely.

We were always wary of rivers at night time as they were infested with spirits from the other side. We were brought up with fear of devils, evil spirits and angels, and many of those superstitions were tied up in religions. It must all seem so silly to anyone reading now. I was from a generation whose parents and grandparents exercised a lot of control over them, compared to a new world of opportunities and experiences of nowadays. Devils became quite the thing for me in my childhood and I can still remember many of the images I saw in churches and in my nightmares.

I did love flowers a great deal, and, as well as the cyclamens I desired from the haunted river, I also adored the wildflowers which grew near the beautiful little church of Saint Irene. The flowers which surrounded it exploded in bursts of colour, and I always wanted to take them home, to put in vases in the house, give to my father, or present them as gifts to other people. When I was about five or six years old, my sister and I were allowed to wander up on the hill, sometimes with friends to gather flowers at St Irene's and it was a lovely thing to do. However, on Sundays, things were different. The priest would go on and on for such a long time while the faithful people listened and bowed. Most of the church services in those days were conducted in mediaeval Greek, not a language many could understand, rather like the speaking of Latin in Catholicism many years ago. It wrapped a cloak of mystery around religion, excluding people in a very real sense while allowing them to wonder at a God whose words were hidden from them by the priest. As I stood or sat there, like the other people, I had no idea what he was saying. My attention, however, was elsewhere.

There was a picture on the right-hand side of the wall in the church with Saint Irene holding the Devil. She was standing and she was suppressing him, holding him down by the horns, preventing him from rising up. The Devil was depicted in the shape of a man but with the form of an animal from the waist down, and a couple of horns on his head. I used to stare at this picture rather than listen to the incomprehensible droning of the priest.

I had nightmares about that devil. I shared a large bedroom with Chrysoula and I remember, in the middle of the night, seeing a devil walking through the door and I was terrified out of my wits. If my father asked me to go in my room, I was so scared, I could not. I thought that the Devil was there for me as I had done something naughty. Nothing specific came to mind, but I was always naughty and he would have been able to get me for something or other if he wanted.

Mother was very religious and had icons in a corner of one room and candles in sconces in a recess in the wall. This is the place we were encouraged to pray. It was Paradise if we were good, and Hell the other way. Neither she nor anyone else would say we were going to Hell, they would say we must be good and we would end up in Paradise. They didn't dwell on the negative, rather we were encouraged towards the good outcome, but we definitely knew what the unspoken alternative was.

Due to our Greek background, a lot of mythology seeped into our lives. I recall one of the stories of King Midas. When Midas had his hair cut by his barber, the man discovered that Midas had the ears of a donkey. He was told not to mention this to anyone but, on his walk home, found that he was bursting with the information and desperately wanted to share it. He opened up a hole and whispered into it, *the king has donkey's ears, has donkey's ears, has donkey's ears*. The barber then put earth over the hole and bamboo shoots sprung up all of a sudden. They whispered in the wind, *Midas has donkey's ears, has donkey's ears, has donkey's ears*. A better known story was about Midas' golden touch: everything he touched turned to gold. In thanks for a favour from Midas, the Greek god Dionysus offered Midas whatever reward he desired. Midas asked that whatever he touched should turn into gold. When he touched his daughter and she turned to a statue of gold Midas came to despise wealth as he could never have or touch anything he loved if it was alive. All of these little myths were to tell us something, they made sure we learned things – with the first one we realised that, if someone told us a secret, we should not immediately go and tell the person down the road what they have said. The Midas touch taught us about greed and about being careful regarding what we desired.

All of this, the devils and the myths, the religion and the tales of old loom large when you are a child. These stories were important to life and they stayed with me. We had a strong sense of history which is understandable when you think of where we were born and the places we loved. History was around us; we were living with it every second of every day. We would be so excited when we found something from the past such as a mosaic floor, or Roman baths carved out of the shore, or old coins which could be found now and again. Archaeology was part of our lives as we could literally touch the past. Our lives were steeped in history and it felt perfectly natural to be part of that.

Women were definitely meant to know their place as wives and mothers, although within those roles they could have some power. When tradition was considered alongside the influence of the church and the superstitions which surrounded us all, there was a clear path to follow. It was never a life I sought for myself. I didn't think it was right that my mother or grandmother should be treated in a lesser way just because they were women, and I knew that I would not be willing to accept it when I grew up. There was something in me, a spark, which knew the life they led was not the life for me. I could also see, in all families not just my own, that sons were accorded much higher status than daughters. Although I accepted that as 'just how it was,' it didn't make me see myself as lesser in any way.

My maternal grandmother didn't have a very good relationship with my Pappous my grandfather – they were very different people. She had her own life on the land, with the goats, the donkeys, and her employees whereas he was out travelling all over the district as he was a headmaster in a few villages. He had his own life, doing what he wanted. Most of the school year saw him staying in areas where he was headmaster, coming home only for summer holidays. He was very interested in archaeology and would often organise digs which would involve other people going with him, often in the middle of the night, to uncover things. He was a spendthrift – with his wife's money – and these digs were expensive.

There was one occasion when he went to Lambousa, 'the Shining City', where it was reputed that everything was made of gold, for one of these excavations. There, he discovered the grave of a Princess, with a crown of golden laurel leaves. It was smuggled out of the country and is actually displayed in the Louvre to this day. Many years ago, I saw it in Paris in the Cypriot section with no name but I knew it had been found by my 'Pappous'. He also found two golden disks which are displayed in the Cyprus archaeological Museum. I guess that even then he operated illegally. He wasn't a recognised archaeologist but he had an obsession with archaeology which involved using a lot of my grandmother's money. This was his passion, but it was funded by her. Although, as I have said, he did not receive all of her wealth upon their marriage, there was still an expectation that he could do what he wanted and that the money would be there for it. Had Stete allowed her husband to manage their affairs, I fear that the money would not have lasted long.

Lambousa was a haven for interesting findings. On occasion, on a walk, you would come across mosaic floors, ancient passages leading to nowhere, the queen's marble baths by the sea, and other remains. This area had its own kingdom and was well populated for centuries but because of earthquakes and lootings from invaders of nearby countries, the inhabitants had to leave behind many of their utensils and household goods and move further up to the foot of the mountains. As a result, Lambousa remained untouched and fell to ruin. The new village of Karavas was formed further up at the foot of the mountain. There was a spring by the sea not far from there and as children we looked for bits of gold in the sand. The local goldsmith was the father of one of my friends and he used to sieve the sand for the gold he needed to make jewellery. It was quite literally a place made of gold and it kept Pappous' interest all of his life.

I spent little time with him – it was my grandmother who drew me to her. As a young girl of five or six years, I would watch Stete working for hours - she would make halloumi), or work in the fields gathering tomatoes, onions, melons or other produce or even deliver a new baby kid, or she would be digging, stoning, or irrigating the fields. Whenever I fell out with my mother, I would escape to Stete and she would look after me in her own strange way, with no need for either of us to talk. When I looked at Stete, I would feel as if my life could be anything. I wouldn't be constricted by 'just' being a girl. I would have it all.

Chapter Seven

Spring was a wonderful time of the year in Cyprus with green, red and yellow colours splashed everywhere. It was always a magical season for me. I loved the fields of poppies, the wild anemones, and cyclamens on the hills. In the valley of flowers, we would always gather great big bunches to take home. With the winter left well behind we would visit Grandmother Eleni that bit more often. Father had property in Lapithos which he wanted to check while we played in the adjacent fields. I can't really remember if I was ever inside my grandmother's house, as we were always told to stay outside. She never showed any emotion or pleasure in seeing us so it seems unlikely that we would be invited inside. We would run about in the front yard and the fields at the side of the house, often playing in the nearby stream for hours. The water was clear and drinkable and such a relief once the scorching summer heat arrived. A few yards further down there was a large reservoir where the water was stored for irrigating the fields in the area. This was yet another dangerous attraction for us – the vast square reservoir was deep with a considerable amount of water. We would often climb up the sides to the top when our father was some distance away and play in the water which was cool and refreshing.

Summer would come in with a bang. Temperatures could soar to 40 degrees Celsius (100°F) and higher, making the heat unbearable especially in July and August. The greatest attraction of summer was the sea. We would go down when the sun was less intense late in the afternoons or early in the morning, walking or catching the bus. We loved the freedom of the various bays, swimming out into the sea for what seemed like miles and taking many chances with our lives despite Mama's warnings. At least twice I nearly drowned. On the first occasion I was standing on a flat rock when the sea suddenly became rough, wave after wave covered me completely and I thought *that's it*. At last, a miracle happened, and the sea became calmer. The second time was much worse. The sea was swollen and rough and the waves were enormous. I went for a swim but, on my way back, became tired and out of breath. I was very frightened. The men sitting at the restaurant above the bay came running down and, with their help, I managed to clamber out and survive. The good times most definitely outweigh the bad. It was fantastic sitting high up at the restaurant at Mare Monte, having something to drink after a swim and chatting to our friends as we watched the sun go down.

Our house was also a wonderland to us children. Over the back and to the left of the house stretched the gardens. There were four large yards surrounding the house which had to be swept and kept clean all the time, and that became one of my jobs as I got older – although I was still very little when I was given such responsibilities. One yard was at the front of the house and at one side of it was the long garage and the old jacaranda tree which always bloomed at Easter time with its bell-like blue flowers. The other side led onto the long drive which took us to the main road. Roughly in the middle of the drive there were steps. Once up half a dozen narrow, earthen steps, a path wound up through lemon and orange groves and took us to the back of one of our neighbour's houses. These people were small, subsistence farmers, as were most people in that area.

Chrysoula and I would often be sent in the evening to a neighbour's house to buy tomatoes, marrows, cucumber, or aubergines, depending on what Mama required. This produce would be displayed in large flat bamboo panniers but to get to it all, we had to enter a large gloomy hall with slabs of marble on the floor. There were no windows, only doors on either side which were normally shut. The large wooden back door was always open but we were quite cautious about entering. The family had a son in his early twenties who had schizophrenia and who was in the habit of exposing himself. He suffered from terrible depression and would get hospitalised now and again, coming back home every so often. The poor man was caught in a never-ending cycle of ill health. He never spoke to anybody but silently wandered about. Sometimes he would pass through my Stete's olive grove walking towards the sea, or he would sit on the steps in the middle of our drive all curled up. I used to get very frightened when returning home if it was getting dark. Although sympathetic, I must confess to being scared of him. There was a profound ignorance then about mental illness and very little in the way of treatment or support for people with mental health issues or their families.

We did wander freely. It was a childhood of independence to a large extent and I always felt welcomed by everyone. Walking through my uncle's field, there was a shortcut in front of the same neighbour's house to one of our friends in the village, Evi, but we rarely took it because there were two very large oxen in the yard. It was a very frightening route to take since we had to squeeze through a narrow space behind or at the front of these enormous beasts. I always avoided this route if I was on my own but with Chrysoula I felt braver.

We were not pampered children. I don't think any children were in those days. We were expected to help out with chores almost from the time we could walk and those were not years of indulgence. Chrysoula and I were expected to look after the younger ones. I developed a good relationship with one of my sisters, Despo who was born when I was seven years old and I claimed her as my own. She became the cleverest one of us all and she was mine really, she would do everything for me and if I wanted anything, she would get it for me. Thea, the youngest one, was closer to Chrysoula. The younger ones didn't work as hard as we had - they had a different upbringing altogether. My father was a very active, demanding man. He wanted everything done and done in absolutely the right way so he had everyone on the go, undertaking things for him. He would never have dreamt of taking on caring duties for any of us, and everything in that department fell to Mother. As there were a lot of us, as well as the house and land to run, it was natural I suppose that she would expect us two older girls to help out with the little ones.

During my early years, Father would come home earlier and take us for a swim down by the monastery but his visits became rarer as more siblings arrived on the scene.

I used to enjoy the visit from the seasonal workers who arrived each autumn. About a dozen of them would come to gather the produce from the fields. They slept upstairs in the various bedrooms as well as spreading their bedding on the large upstairs square veranda at the back of the house. They played with me when I was young, put me on their knee and sang to me. They were great fun and I missed them terribly when they left. As a working child myself, I helped gather the almonds and lemons, working just as hard as the others. After a windfall there would be masses of olives under the olive trees and I would accompany Mama to collect them, soon becoming itchy, hot and uncomfortable as ants crawled up my skin. I was always willing, always happy to work – especially if I could add to my piggy bank savings. The greatest motivator of all! The only task I detested was the cleaning of the vine leaves from around the bunches of grapes – coming across large green or brown caterpillars was a nightmare to me due to my phobia.

Although much of my time was spent roaming around the area where we lived and doing a lot of work for such a little girl, the influence of some other members of my family was a strong and constant presence in my life. My Pappous was a serious and formal man, feared and respected by us as children. I remember his booming voice so clearly. His sister Eleni, my great aunt, married and settled in Nicosia. She had a large family of boys and one girl, also called Maria. The family became well known in Nicosia as one of the sons started the Loizides College and my cousin Andreas Alexander had taken over the management due to the premature death of the founder. The Loizides brothers were also known for the establishment of travel and tourism offices. Aunt Eleni and Maria visited us often in Karavas and I was particularly interested in my great aunt's painted glass eye. Pappous' youngest brother settled in Larnaca with his wife and daughter, Claire, who was about my own age. She was always fashionably dressed but I thought rather snobby. One of Pappous's brothers, Christos was a record-breaking athlete in running in Cyprus but, unfortunately, his talent didn't pass down to mother's family.

By this time, I was at school. My first day had been seen as a very important event – Mama lit a candle for the day whilst I was away and only when I came back home did she blow it out. My first day was really quite odd, I remember running about in a big yard at the back of the school and sitting with some children at the top, but I felt very strange, it felt peculiar to be away from my home and my family. It must have felt unusual to Mama too as, had she been allowed to continue to work as a teacher, it would have been her first day of the school year as well. Chrysoula had started two years before. I don't remember missing her much, although quite close in age we seemed to lead independent lives at that age.

My life was school, work, and Church – albeit with a lot of play and adventure scattered throughout my days. We were asked to pray a lot, every night, before bed, and to go to Church each Sunday. Sometimes, I would say, 'Oh dear, I cannot go, I feel unwell,' but my mother was not easily fooled and I usually had to attend. I remember sometimes having swollen eyes due to too much sleep and I would rub them even more so that I didn't have to go. It even worked sometimes! We went to the church service so terribly early that I was always tired even at the thought. I would rather stay in bed than go. Mama made a good effort with our special Sunday clothes. We were taken to a seamstress in the village to have them professionally made. We had to be very respectable, especially on a Sunday. Like Papa, Mama always liked to dress herself properly at all times. I remember often going to that seamstress and sitting as she and Mama looked at patterns and talked about material. Fashion was a great interest of hers and she passed that onto us all, teaching me how to knit and helping me make my first cardigan when I was five. It was purple with pink stripes. When she didn't have to attend to the fields she would spend most of her morning embroidering, crocheting and mending. Some of my clothes were passed down from Chrysoula, but they were beautifully altered by either Mama or the seamstress. My school uniform had to be kept on at all times during the school term as our school believed that, if you went anywhere after school to the village, your uniform represented you. You had to even keep your hat on.

On Christmas Day, we had to wear something new – we didn't get the huge quantity of presents children receive nowadays. I sometime think that this abundance is overwhelming for children and often ruinous for parents. I usually received new socks or something to wear for the day. Unfortunately, Mama would sometimes get the wrong size of socks and I would be very disappointed, but I still struggled to wear them as they were new after all. Christmas was quite a modest affair in those days. In Cyprus, it wasn't celebrated with bright lights and tinsel-covered trees, street decorations and cards. I remember being dragged out of my warm bed at an unearthly hour, maybe 4am, to attend the early Mass at the local parish church in the centre of the village, and this was not an occasion I could ever escape. With bleary eyes, we would dress ourselves in our best Sunday clothes, always finding my new, too-small socks, the heel part under my foot. The church was always full to overflowing during this time, full of the once-a-year churchgoers paying their respects to the occasion. It was a terribly long service, typical of Greek Orthodox events. After a short while, all I wanted to do was close my eyes and drift into a dreamland despite my mother's protestations. She would attentively listen to the long sermon, as would the rest of the women in the female part of the congregation. She would cross herself many times, and with only her lips moving, recite after the priest and the two hymn singers (two men who would stand in their own pulpits opposite each other at the front of the church).

My father was not a believer in the slightest – he would stand with the men on the right-hand side of the Church which was reserved for the males, patiently tolerating the long service but looking forward to having his special Christmas breakfast. This often included pickled small birds and morsels of unleavened bread. The Christmas dinner was truly something else – the turkey, who had wandered carefree in our large garden since spring - was sacrificed for the occasion, with Chrysoula and I howling at the injustice. I remember having the young turkey come to stay with us every spring as a guest for many years. He would run about in the garden like the rest of us, amongst the bright yellow flowers and forget-me-nots. We would make mounds with the lemongrass and play for hours, rolling, tumbling and making a lot of noise. Those early years were so much fun – and I am sure the turkey enjoyed his days of freedom before his inevitable demise at Christmas.

My mother would carefully prepare and cook that turkey, all day it seemed, along with delicious roasted Cyprus potatoes. My father would carve the roasted bird, filled with home-made stuffing, and all of us, without exception, would devour everything in front of us giving praise to the cook. The Christmas pudding followed the British tradition; spirit was poured over it and set alight prior to eating. I was always rather disappointed when I tasted it and I would rather have had the special Cyprus sweets made with filo pastry and crushed almonds and drizzled with syrup.

The Christmas socks would have come from one of the people who came around the houses with small wares for sale. From Panayiota, the vagabond lady who visited with her bundle of wares and various goods, and from some other traders. A man on a donkey with things piled up on it, sold cloth and ribbons. If we needed a big item such as a raincoat for walking to school, Papa and Mama would go shopping on Ledra Street, the main street of Nicosia, and we would be left in the back of the car to wait for them. That was normal then, just leaving their children to wait and assuming all would be well and for us, fortunately, it always was. When very young, I would often fall asleep but I could hear the hooves of the horses and carriages running along the cobbled streets of Nicosia as my parents did the shopping.

One day, when I was seven and despite Mama's objections, I took my new bicycle on an errand down the hill to a café where I needed to buy bread. I was only just learning and had no idea how to work the brakes. I approached a junction, went over the main road, and with great force, crashed into the café wall. My shiny bike was completely mangled and my heart was ready to break. I was covered in cuts and bruises but it could have been much worse. A group of men had been sitting chatting and drinking coffee – to my amazement, they came to my rescue and straightened my bicycle. Amongst them was one of my primary school teachers, Mr Vakis, who lived nearby. I was so frightened of the consequences but they did such a good job mending it that, shaken, I managed to buy the bread and hurry back home, pretending nothing had happened. Pappous had picked up half a story and came up the drive shouting, 'Kassandra! Kassandra! Are the children at home? Are they alright? There has been an accident in the village!' I ran away, hid for a while behind some bushes until he left. Miraculously, I was never found out. Another adventure for little Maro!

⸺⟨◈⟩⸺

Chapter Eight

On the outskirts of Karavas and Kyrenia, there were two large buildings inhabited by Assyrian families reputed to be of royal blood and in exile. The family that lived in Karavas kept very much to themselves; only the two younger girls, who must have been in their late teens, mixed with the locals. They both befriended my cousins who were of similar age and much older than us. One of them, Virginia, ran the Brownies (along with my cousin) in the village which Chrysoula and I attended. During the summer we would go camping up on the Troodos mountains where Guides and Brownies came from all over Cyprus. The bugle call to the colours would be heard early in the morning, quite an eerie sound amongst the whispering pine trees and with the sun just appearing over the tips of the mountains and through the pine trees. During the day we would visit the nearby mountain villages and make friends with young members from other parts of Cyprus. At night, there was a camp fire we would all gather round, drinking cocoa and singing songs. It was indeed a very enjoyable summer break and there was no sign at that point that my life would ever be anything other than a series of happy events, safe in the bosom of a loving family.

My father was away all day long looking after his car business in Kyrenia. He would come home quite late in the evenings, bleary eyed, and when we were all ready for bed. He was a man who really looked after himself and cared about his appearance, always wearing suits which were tailor-made at the best establishments. Quite often we would wait so that we could all have supper together and often we would simply not be allowed to eat until he got there, striding in, so well-dressed and commanding respect. A notion of the 'man of the house' certainly prevailed in those days. My father was always tired, he would often talk about his business to my mother, telling her what had happened that day. I would be listening most of the time, sometimes getting quite upset with what I was hearing. For instance, his cars would be crashed by somebody who had hired them or people would run away without paying the full charge.

Our house was large and Mama maximised its potential by renting out the upstairs floor to families for long lets. This was of added interest to me as I enjoyed getting to know other people and having some attention from them. A number of the tenants became friends for many years to come. A couple of times we had English families staying there and although rather difficult to interact with, they created an interest. There was once a single parent Englishwoman, Mrs Forbes, with a young girl called Chloe who must have been about three years of age. She would often be strapped by her mother on the railings of the balcony in the early hours of the morning, screaming and crying until the child carer, a woman from the village came up to rescue her and look after her for the rest of the day. The carer, a mother of 12 herself, was tearful when telling my mother about Chloe. My mother was also very upset about it However, the mysterious Englishwoman did not stay at our house for very long and we children thought maybe she was a spy. This was all terribly interesting to me and I must admit that I enjoyed the drama.

One family who had a great impact on our lives was the Seligmans who returned on numerous occasions. They were a very artistic family. Adrian Seligman was a writer whose books were about the villagers of Cyprus. His wife Rosemary was an artist who used to sketch the illustrations in his books. Rosemary was the daughter of Arthur Grimble who had been the Governor of the Seychelles and who was also a well known writer.

Rosemary Seligman was very pretty with blonde hair, tall and slim, quietly spoken and of calm disposition. She was an 'English rose.' Rosemary spoke only a little Greek but somehow seemed to understand all that was said. I was probably about eight years old when she first put the seed in my mind of being a physiotherapist, albeit indirectly. I remember her standing on the balcony speaking to my mother with me lingering near the lily pond listening to every word.

'Perhaps Chrysoula would benefit from a physiotherapist,' she said, referring to my sister's right arm. 'It is such a pity that there is no one here to provide some assistance.'

At the time there were no physiotherapists in Cyprus although there was clearly a need for them. Rosemary's comment made me sit up and think – if there was something that I could do, something I could work at as an adult, and no one else was doing it, that would give me great standing, would it not? It was something that Rosemary had clearly thought of too.

'Maybe it is something that Maro would consider when she is older? I think she would have the temperament and she is clearly a clever girl.' I was quite a physical child, keen on sport and exercise and for that reason she believed that training and working as a physio would be a good idea. Many years later, I was taken with the idea of becoming a geographer but it never materialised. The idea of physiotherapy as mentioned by Rosemary when I was eight was reignited and I went on to study that.

Adrian and Rosemary had a little boy of about three years called Simon. He was a very intelligent child with blonde tousled hair, who was looked after by the same woman who had cared for poor Chloe. Andrew and Rosemary were good parents, unlike Mrs Forbes, and definitely not spies. I was very disappointed when they decided to rent another house near Kyrenia. Their new accommodation was a few miles away from Karavas. It was a larger house which they needed since by now they had they had another child called Matthew. They had a large garden and a pony for their little boy running about – we often visited them there and they were always pleased to see us.

I can recall some other tenants staying at the house – one of the families came from Paphos, they were a policeman's family. The father was tall and well-built, with three daughters and one son. The son, Harry, was my own age but deaf and non-verbal. He was rather hyperactive and we would constantly have fights. He was intelligent but, being unable to communicate, we ended up screaming and in tears as if we were both wild animals. The three girls were quite a few years older than I. After a little while, the family moved further along to a roomier house but we still kept in touch. We would sit on their balcony when we visited, overlooking the main road of the village, sipping Greek coffee and having some of the special Cypriot sweets they made.

There was another policeman's family staying in the upper floor but I remember very little about them. However, I do recall a Polish family, Paul and Maroula, and their two children, as well as Paul's brother Tibby and his daughter Kozima. Maroula originally came from Nicosia where she was a hairdresser and Paul's mother was one of the clients she regularly visited at her house. Apparently, Paul's mother was a very difficult lady but somehow Maroula, being very patient and good natured, managed to cope with her. Paul was so impressed that he decided she would be a good wife. They had a little baby girl, Angela, and a little boy, Peter of about three. Tibby had been married but was now divorced from a cabaret lady with whom he had his daughter. Kozima must have been fourteen or fifteen when they stayed with us and could speak a few languages. She was planning to become a pilot. Much to the disapproval of those around her, she had a boyfriend a few years older than her, the son of the local priest. Maroula and my mother were forever gossiping about them. Their relationship was contrary to the norms and culture of the village but Kozima, her father and uncle seemed oblivious to all of that. Paul had an vintage ex-post office car and was very proud of it. He would often pile all the children into it and take us to the seaside. He was a very caring man to everyone. He and his brother were musicians, both playing in a band at Zephryos, the local nightclub. Paul played the bassoon and Tibby the saxophone.

It is so strange that these people have stayed in my mind over all of these years. The memories of childhood are vivid and real, all of my senses return to Karavas when I think of my childhood, and the people who populated my life are as clear to me today as they were over seventy years ago. There were, however, great changes coming my way which would alter my life completely.

At the age of seven, all of us apart from my father went to live in the high mountain village of Vasilia. Vasilia means the Kingdom of the Kings, and it was to be our home for a year. My mother became a teacher there, taking me with her as well as my younger sister Despo (who was a baby), Chrysoula, and my brother Andreas. Vasilia was an amazingly beautiful village at the foot of a five peak mountain (Pentadactylos) overlooking the northern part of Cyprus. To this day, I am not certain why she decided to just pack and go. Mama had never taught for a sustained period as she had so many of her own children right away after marriage and she certainly would not have been able to work as a teacher outside of the home when we were all very small. I don't know what made her decide to leave Karavas and go to Vasilia to teach, but she did – I also don't know why it was suddenly seen as acceptable. Maybe she felt it was her last chance to fulfil her lifelong ambition to practice her teaching or perhaps my parents had fallen into some financial difficulties and she needed to earn. I never asked her, and I'll never know.

Papa stayed behind but would collect us over the weekend and take us back to our village. I hated going back as the house had to be cleaned before we could settle each weekend. It looked sad, empty and neglected having been left unattended over the week. The leaves from the Virginia Creeper would pile in the backyard and have to be swept by us as soon as we got there, almost a symbol of the neglect that part of our life was experiencing.

In Vasilia, there were two schools, divided by age, and Mama took charge of the school attended by the younger ones. I was in Primary 2 when we left which meant that Mama was in charge of my year and now my teacher. The other school was further down the road from ours and the teacher there was male. I had an amazing, carefree life in Vasilia, which was an idyllic place. The school was situated in a lovely spot up on the mountains, a beautiful place for gathering flowers, where I could wander about whenever I had time. As one of the village teachers, Mama was treated very well and people had a lot of time for me as I was a very friendly, curious child who would freely pop in and out of their houses. They were not used to that up on the mountains, up on the hills but they opened their hearts to me.

It was rather strange to have Mama as my teacher, but she certainly didn't treat me any better than the other children. On our first day, we were allocated our seats, and this was the privilege of the teacher, as always.

'Maro, you will sit next to Elenitsa,' she told me.

'No,' I immediately replied.

She glared at me and repeated her demand. 'Maro – you *will* sit next to Elenitsa.'

'No. No I will not,' I told her. 'She is a peasant. I do not want to sit beside her.' Elenitsa was actually a lovely little girl with rosy cheeks and auburn hair, and I was not being nice at all.

'I will ask you one last time. Sit there,' said Mama.

'I will not.'

'Then come down here to the front of the class.'

I walked down with the rest of the girls and boys watching me, expecting to be given a telling off. Instead, Mama belted me on my bottom. There was no special treatment – or maybe that was special. Maybe she would not belt another child. I still feel the overwhelming resentment towards my mother when she gave me the belt for that, and the embarrassment mixed with humiliation of being chastised in such a way. Of course, I had my own ideas as to who I wanted to sit next to and I felt it very unfair that she should force me to sit next to a peasant girl. I was quite a popular child with others of my own age and with adults despite all of my failings, and I probably used that popularity for my own gains. Sadly for me, it did not work on that occasion but perhaps that was for the best.

My days in Vasilia were wonderful. I had a joyful life of freedom at this picturesque village in Northern Cyprus. Sometimes, under my mother's orders, I would take my classmates all the way through the village, down to the other school for a nature lesson. It was great fun and I enjoyed the responsibility; I would put them in a line, two by two, with me standing outside the line, shouting orders at them to keep them in position. I was quite the little dictator, taking them all the way down to the other school and I felt like I had really found my calling in life. If anybody dared to get out of line, I would be furious. I was autocratic and I loved it. It was another strange contradiction within me – I was wild, but I was also responsible or at least determined that no-one else would be wild when I was in charge.

My school was an old, one large-roomed building built high up into the rocks with a small playground at the front, also carved out of the hill. After descending a dozen steps or so there was a narrow earthen road leading to the village and the valley below. Our house consisted of two rooms and a tiny bedroom, a hall and a very small kitchen. We originally went there in the autumn when the school term started. I just loved it. I cannot recall the winter but I do remember the spring when I would watch the house martins for hours, flying here and there into the eaves of our house, feeding their young ones. I would sit on the doorstep, overlooking the mountain slopes, relishing the warmth of the spring sun and inhaling the pure, fresh mountain air. We would often climb onto the slopes and gather bunches of spring flowers such as hyacinths, cyclamens, and anemones, all growing wild in clusters.

At times, we would visit some of the locals with my mother when she wasn't teaching. One family was some distance away in a house tucked high up at the side of the mountain. They lived in a long building, quite austere and bare, surrounded by a large clearing and surrounded by mountains. I was very sad one day when I heard that a young Turkish girl had dropped to her death from those mountains trying to rescue her goat. I often looked up at the sheer drop where she came to the end of her life and felt a chill run through me. The villagers were very hospitable, many of them would offer us walnuts, which I particularly loved, with local mountain honey, scented with thyme and other herbs, as well as traditional Cyprus sweets.

One of the highlights during our time there was the wedding of the daughter of the mayor of the village. It was amazing, like a real-life Big Fat Greek Wedding. They lived in a huge, rich house with many outbuildings further down the village where the wedding went on and on for days. There was so much to eat and drink and so much preparation had gone into it all that it was quite staggering. During the preparation, I would go into the kitchens and watch the cooks getting the delicious traditional dishes ready, slowly cooking in the ovens, lamb, pastitsions, moussakas, trifles and all sorts of traditional Greek Cypriot sweets and pastries. I would wander freely amongst everybody. They were all welcoming and made a fuss of me, which I loved. I was a confident, outgoing child and everyone seemed to like me. Occasions such as this reinforced for me the feeling that my life was blessed and always would be.

Sometimes, in the middle of the week, my father would visit us but I was quite indifferent to his presence. The only thing I liked about his arrival was that I would be sent to have a sleepover at a neighbour's house further up the hill at the back of our house. The old lady – who was called Eleni just like my paternal grandmother - used to dress in a very traditional way, with a black headscarf, a long skirt down to her ankles, a long-sleeved shirt and heavy boots. I saw many such women - they were typical of their place and time. This woman was tall, thin and pleasant. She would look after my baby sister Despo when my mother was at work and was always pleased to have me staying when father visited. Eleni's daughter, son-in-law, and grandsons were away in Nicosia most of the time – the boys went to school there and I believe the parents had jobs there too. Now and again, they would come back to the house in Vasilia and that is when I would see them. Again, everyone made a fuss of me and I felt very special.

Eleni stayed in a small attic room filled with a huge, low double bed and a dressing table. The space in front of the bed and the dressing table was very small but the cramped conditions did not upset me. She would settle me in the big double bed, always being careful not to knock my head on the ceiling above – it was very cosy and comfortable and I loved the attention. The old lady looked after me very well and spoke to me about her family while we cosied up, especially about her Granddaughter Yianoula for whom she was knitting a thick woolly jumper with lambs wool gathered from the mountain slopes.

My days in Vasilia truly were magical and I will never forget them, but time marches on and we could not stay there forever. Again, I had no idea why decisions were made and changes occurred yet again, I was only a child and children were not involved in such discussions in those days, but, sadly, our time there would soon be over and I would regret that very much.

A year of my life in Vasilia seemed a long time. I believe a year when six or seven years old is equivalent to five years of an adult's life. It certainly added to my experiences and helped in enriching my life.

Chapter Nine

After our stay in Vasilia, we went back to Karavas. It was a beautiful interlude in our lives. I entered the third year of the local primary school and that's when I met Popi, my lifelong friend who was a year older than me. She was a new pupil and was sitting directly behind me. We became inseparable, studying and eating together. We were with each other all day long. Popi was full of personality and fun. She was talkative with good social skills and developed into a beautiful girl.

People come into your life for a reason, whether it is for a season or a lifetime. Popi has been my support and confidante for life and I would never have known that when we met as children. The large Damianos family was well known in Karavas and her father had several brothers. One of them competed relentlessly against my Uncle Panayiotis for the position of Mayor. This was quite a political battle each time, however Uncle Panayiotis would always succeed. He was repeatedly re-elected and was probably the longest serving mayor of Karavas. The competition between our uncles however never interfered in our friendship. Neither Popi nor I ever mentioned the fight and remained the best of friends.

I must be honest and say that I had a very good childhood despite the discipline and the superstitions. It was perfect really as I lived in Paradise. When I returned from Vasilia, I slipped back into my old life quite easily, although I did miss what we'd had for that year. I had my walks on the hills, I scampered up onto the mountains, I wandered to a church cut out of the rocks – it was a beautiful life. During the summer holidays, I would gather flowers which bloomed everywhere, I would spend time with friends in the morning then go for a swim in the afternoon in the stunning clear water. We would dry by the sun and go back home again We would look for shells, throw stones in the sea, and there was a sense of safety, of just being able to be a child. There was no feeling of danger apart from nature; the river and the snakes were threats but people did not seem to be.

Even as a very young child, I was allowed to wander off by myself. I would go to the foot of the mountain, which was quite a distance, to visit this woman who would go out of her way to make me treacle donuts (Dourkelouthia). They were wonderful and I loved it. Other people used to look after me when I called on them as I was the daughter of Kassandra and everyone knew her. I had some status; I was always welcomed. It was a different time and people in the area always had an open home.

I often used to visit my Aunt Ophelia who was a special influence in my life as she was more serious and had a different personality to my mother. We thought of her as very 'posh'. She was an extremely tidy and very refined woman whose house was 'just so' whereas ours was open to everyone. We had hens and goats, fields and lots of children, a chaotic life whereas hers was very controlled.

Many people in my family were particular in their way of doing things. Aunt Ophelia, for instance, was almost obsessive in her tidiness. Others in the family had rigid views that would not be changed, which could never be altered no matter what. My grandmother's sister, Maria, had a child out of wedlock and this was virtually unheard of back then. I didn't know her but I heard stories of how she was disowned by her parents (my great grandparents). She married the father of her baby but unfortunately died in childbirth. Her parents didn't even go to the funeral. They were very hard-hearted people.

There were similar constraints for my generation. A sense of propriety pervaded everything. I did have a friend who was a boy but that was not really allowed. You never kissed or held hands: that would never happen and, they were not boyfriends in the real sense. I never heard of anyone getting rid of a baby they didn't want but these things happen everywhere and always have so I'm sure it did occur, but it would have been such a source of shame that it would never be discussed. For us as children, much of life was hidden in silent looks and hushed whispers.

I did a lot of naughty things in my childhood, quite idiotic in some ways to be honest. We were left to roam free as my mother always had another child to bring up and, in retrospect, I know now that she would also have the worry of ill sons as well. I would go off and do my own thing, often without any siblings or friends, and felt welcome everywhere. When I visited people, they would go out of their way to make things for me which I adored. I was very indulged. On very hot days, any child would get fed up lying down and having a siesta. It is all very well for grown-ups to nap for an hour or two, but we would wander off.

Once I was with my sister Chrysoula and we went a couple of miles down the road towards the sea where there was a reservoir – this reservoir belonged to Kyrios Takis. He had a little hut there amongst his lemon groves and, on this afternoon, he was having his siesta too. We looked at this very inviting reservoir and it seemed so big to us little children – we peered inside and the water wasn't really up to the top, so we climbed over and went inside, had a swim, kept looking out for Mr Takis, then we got out and ran home. The thought of that now is quite chilling. For all of those little children to take such a risk when there was no adult to see or hear them if they got into trouble could have been deadly. We didn't care – the days were long and hot, the grown-ups were napping, and we had the world at our feet.

Once when I was ten, a friend of mine invited me to go for a swim. Swimming in itself was not unusual, we all had plenty of opportunities, but this day would push the boundaries a little further. My friend Georgia said, 'My sister Eleni will be there too, so there will be someone to watch us.'

Mama gave in when I told her about Eleni and was happy enough that it would just be us three girls. We had arranged to meet at my grandmother's olive grove, taking the path and the road to the sea, but when I got there, not only were Georgia and Eleni waiting, but also an older male cousin.

'Oh dear,' I said, 'my mother will not like this. What age is he?' I asked my friend.

'He is very old,' she said with the assurance of a child thinking that anyone more than a few years older is positively decrepit. 'I think he is 19 – or maybe even 20.'

'My mother would not want me to go anywhere with him,' I repeated, and it was true. My friend had never told me he would be there, and it would not have been acceptable – even going with my own male cousin at that age would not have been deemed proper. It was just the way that boys and girls did not associate in that manner. Any associations with the opposite sex were forbidden – marriages were arranged in those days and the bride had to remain a virgin, although men did not. Georgia managed to convince me, and we went for a swim in this idyllic little place called Varkouthes (the Place of the Small Barge). There were fishing huts with nets drying at the front. There was a little well three or four yards away from where the sea water came, with beautiful fresh water. This was very unusual, and when we were very little, my mother used to walk us down there and let us swim, come out, and she would then immerse us in the water of the well. It was so fresh and good, to wash away the salt. Then she would give us pieces of bread, halloumi, tomatoes, cucumber and olives which I adored. It was a really charming place, with a few boats moored along the front.

I was happy to be there as the place had lovely memories. However, on this occasion, I was already being bold by being in the company of the young man, and when I was encouraged to go in even further to swim, I felt that I would do that too. I was breaking one rule, so why not chance my luck even more? I was a strong swimmer at that age and needed no help but, for some reason, on the way out into deeper water, the boy caught hold of my ankle. Perhaps he was just having fun or perhaps he thought I could not swim well, but, my goodness, I thought he was sexually harassing me! I could not have been more shocked by his touch if he had pinched my bottom. I was really quite upset about it but didn't say much. I let it happen and certainly never told my mother. It felt like a huge secret even although in retrospect it was nothing at all.

One day in my first year at the Gymnasium, a girl in my sister's year at school, Sotiroula, passed me a note from a boy called Peter. I was terribly excited when I opened it, even more so when I read that he was declaring undying feelings of love for me. This letter was thrilling. I was well aware that girls were forbidden to have anything to do with the opposite sex. My neighbour Stavros became his friend. They were in the same year at school and very soon after that note, we started meeting by the wall at the end of our long garden.

Stavros and Peter would sit in the clearing at the end of Stavros's lemon grove making a noise, talking and laughing until I appeared over the wall which separated our property.

Meeting a boy was a big secret in those days and we were not supposed to have any association with the opposite sex even just as friends. I had known Peter for a couple of years – he was older than me by a year. We never held hands or kissed – that was strictly forbidden. He had a sister, Avgi, who was older than me by two years and was in Chrysoula's class at school. During the week, they lived in a rented flat in Lapithos where the gymnasium was. They both would go home over the weekend as their father ran a small grocery shop in a nearby village and Peter had to help on Saturdays. They were very poor and could hardly make ends meet. There were occasions when he couldn't pay the nominal annual fee of £12.00 at the Gymnasium and he would have been thrown out if it wasn't for the PE teacher who paid the fee so he could stay. Ironically, given her romantic history, Mama would not have entertained for a second the idea of my having a relationship with someone of Peter's background. She had been very clear that, when the time came, I needed to marry a man of status. Perhaps her own experience with my father and the difficulties this had caused within her family had coloured her thinking, but I believe it was probably just the general adherence to rigid social structures at that time. Everyone had their place in society and that was considered the most important thing of all when it came to relationships.

In my heart of hearts, I never did take Peter seriously. Mother had instilled different ideas in my mind and the man of my future had to be educated and from a good family background. The beliefs instilled in childhood and youth are hard to dislodge and it is difficult to overcome the convictions that lay deep within us. After a little while, my parents received an anonymous letter from someone telling them about me having a boyfriend but fortunately nothing was found. Some letters I had were hidden in between the pages of my books – I denied everything. I was made to swear on the Bible that I did not have a boyfriend as the letter alleged. However, our relationship continued as before, meeting in secret. At the beginning of our friendship, Peter gave me a gift of a book, 'Wuthering Heights' by Charlotte Bronte. The poor boy must have spent money he didn't really have to give me such a gift.

Though always an avid reader I was put in a terrible quandary regarding the book in that I couldn't take it home to read in secret as Mother could spot it and start asking how it came into my possession. I threw it away before getting home and a few days later I bought the same book from the Kyrenia bookshop so that I could read it but secure in the knowledge that it had come into my hands 'morally'. I loved that book. I read it in Greek and English and also saw the film twice. It was indeed ironic, our relationship in years to come became complex and unequal, in some ways resembling that of Heathcliff and Cathy's doomed love, lost potential and wasted passion. There were other boys interested but none as daring, intense and lasting as Peter.

These notions of who was an appropriate suitor, or even an appropriate friend, permeated all of our lives. There were very clear demarcation lines regarding what was seen as appropriate behaviour, passed down from generation to generation.

My grandmother Despina was very wealthy but quite miserly and, she only showed generosity to her son, Panayiotis. When he successfully finished his studies and opened a business as a dentist, he was even more wonderful in her eyes than he had ever been. As I have said, sons always took precedence over daughters and the fact that people would travel for miles, waiting for hours, to see her son the dentist, made Despina madly proud. However, he was not only in demand as a dentist but as a bachelor. He eventually married Augousta, a beautiful young woman, also a dentist, from Nicosia, who was at least twelve years his junior.

Augousta was seen as a suitable daughter-in-law and she knew exactly how to get around my grandmother who amongst other things gave her a pair of rare and valuable Byzantine earrings. Uncle Panayiotis was also helped to build a magnificent house in a plot next to Auntie Ophelia, whose home was nowhere near as grand. The basement of the house was eventually occupied by grandmother when her sight was failing some years later. I would take her down in the dark after seeing to her animals in the field above our house. I was frightened of the dark and always relieved when Chrysoula came along.

As time went on, Auntie Ophelia and her family became very important to us. During the summer holidays, my sister and I would visit her daily. She was always happy to see us. In the late afternoons and early evenings, we would sit on the veranda at the front of the house and watch the people in their best clothes passing by for their evening stroll with groups of friends all laughing and joking. The street at the front of her house would be empty during the week but absolutely packed full over the weekend. Everyone was out for a stroll, everyone wanted to be seen.

Ophelia had trained as a teacher, just like Mama, but she never worked. Her husband, Uncle Alexander was a teacher too. My cousins were a good bit older than me and Chrysoula, the three daughters by many years, but we were still very close. Andreas the youngest of their children was still eight years my senior and my favourite. He had a non-identical twin, Pambos. The story was, when the twins were little, lightning came down and struck Pambos as he lay in the cot, leaving him mentally and physically affected. It didn't, however, hit the other twin who lay beside him. This was clearly an invention but gave the family a 'reason' for what was seen as a shameful thing. Pambos was kept out of sight in the basement and was looked after mainly by his paternal grandmother. If he came to the front of the house, he would be told to go away to the back of the house. Shocking though this is to us now, this was quite common in those days. Any disabilities were kept quiet for shame and embarrassment. With the scientific and genetic knowledge, I now have I would say that Pambos was probably afflicted by the syndrome which afflicted my brothers too. A random genetic defect, the curse of my family, passed on through the female line.

Andreas, my cousin, was full of fun, he was the one who would instruct me in the latest dances that he picked up in Athens as a student. Rock and roll, cha cha, and others were all practised in the large hall with sparkly, coloured tiles on the floor. Nicos, Andreas' older brother by three years, was very good at maths and taught me during the holidays. Eventually he made mathematics a career.

Just above the sofa hung a large picture of Venice and the canals, people and gondolas, a reminder of Despina's roots. Aunt Euthania's drawing room - or saloni - was kept for special occasions just like the one at our house. Many a time after visiting my auntie, I would go back home and wash and clean the large marble tiles in our hall but I couldn't get them to shine like hers. She was very prim and proper, extremely house-proud, and we were never able to match those incredibly high standards.

Ophelia had a beautiful grey, long haired Persian cat whilst we just had wild cats running around in the field, about seven of them. She also had Lixis, an off-white poodle.

Lixis was a very friendly dog and was always upset to see me and my sister go home. He would stand high up on the river embankment and bark and bark until we disappeared out of sight. Sometimes in the quietness of the night we would still hear him barking even when we reached home about three quarters of a mile away through the olive groves. We had two young mongrel dogs, Scrubby a brown Labrador cross, and Bobbi, a collie cross and whilst Lixis was a well-groomed house dog, ours were outside guard dogs. We loved them both dearly but unfortunately, they had to be shot as rabies was spreading like wildfire in the village. Mother would repeatedly ask us not to go near any of the village dogs because of the disease. Ever since, I have been a little wary of dogs, especially when they jump up to me.

As I have mentioned, Ophelia was very different to my mother, and not just in looks, but personality too. She loved her garden and worked in it constantly. I particularly liked the bed of violets at the front of the house and the profusion of flowers at the side and back. There were pots of carnations on every step of the stairs going up at the back of the house and on the balcony facing the lemon grove.

My father wouldn't have anything to do with Aunt Ophelia and Uncle Alexander or their children. They had never accepted him and had put every possible obstruction in his path to prevent his marriage to Ophelia's sister. Sadly, these fences were never mended. That was indeed a shame as I was very fond of all of them. All of these memories, all of these thoughts, show just how important some social structures were at that time and place. Times would change, everything would change, but, for now, what was seen as right and what was seen as proper mattered almost more than anything.

Chapter Ten

I was popular at school and my schoolwork was always good. I had an A at the end of each year of primary but now the time had come to leave and go to the Lapithos gymnasium. This was two or three miles walking distance from my house. During some of the winter downpours my father would give us a lift in his car before he went to work – he would often also call to collect Mr Pashios the English language teacher who lived on the outskirts of the village and who would normally cycle.

The gymnasium was a long, symmetrical building with the entrance in the middle, painted in the Greek colours of white and blue. It sat high above the main road, surrounded by large playing fields. Most of the teachers came from the mainland, only one or two were locals, one of whom was the PE teacher who was mentioned earlier in connection with my elder sister and her disability. The other was a teacher of English, not Mr Pashios, but a particular teacher who couldn't control the class at all. On one occasion, he completely lost his head and started hitting the students, randomly striking out at whoever happened to be sitting in front of him – including me. I was well behaved and took this demonstration of aggression rather badly. I got up and walked to the end of the classroom, opened the door and marched straight to the headmaster's office. I knocked on the door and told him all about what had happened. He listened carefully, thanked me and said he would deal with the situation. The teacher improved his way of teaching and the episode was not repeated again.

I particularly liked physics and the teacher who taught it was a good one. Miss Campa and Miss Costopoulou were my favourite teachers of all. They were friends from Athens, and with tears in their eyes they would talk about the atrocities of the Civil War in Greece. They obviously had lived through some horrendous times and experiences. They were both very kind to me – one taught us modern Greek and the other Classics. Near Christmas, they would organise a show in the theatre in Lapithos. I recall standing in front of the drawn curtains. The stage seemed so high above the auditorium packed with people. My heart beat fast as I had a vision of falling face down into the audience. I prayed to St Mary asking her not to let me fall and my prayer was answered, not a pin could be heard drop as I recited a very long poem. It was well received and the audience clapped for what seemed a long time. Miss Campa was very complimentary about my performance giving me a big hug when I reached the bottom of the few steps from the stage. It was an exhilarating moment and made me realise that public speaking was not to be feared.

Things were changing for me on a personal level. During my earlier years, I was plump, or tubby as my older cousin Evi would refer to me. I loved nuts, we had almond trees all around our few acres of garden and also walnut trees and I would eat them all day long, along with bananas, tangerines, plums and more. However, I remember losing a considerable amount of weight after a tonsil operation. I shared a room with my father at the time at a private clinic in Kyrenia. I do know now that getting tonsils removed later in life is much worse but at the time, with the solipsism of youth, I thought my father was making a great deal of fuss. My mother during her visits would try to take care of him, giving me very little attention. The operation was a horrendous experience. I remember sitting in a dentist's chair draped with white sheets, aware of what was going on around me and having my tonsils removed under a local anaesthetic. The taste of blood was ghastly. The idea of ice cream over the next few days was of no consolation – one would think I would be put off hospitals forever after such an experience, so it is ironic that I ended up working in them for over forty years. However, one good thing came out of the whole thing. I lost some of my childhood chubbiness. I remember wearing my lovely yellow silk dress and twirling round and round with its full skirt. I started becoming aware of my figure by the time I was 13, going on 14 years old and I was feeling pleased with my looks. The same cousin who had referred to me as tubby said, 'My goodness Maro, you have an amazing figure with a waist like a ring.' I was pleased with her compliment but I was particularly pleased with the attention I was getting from the opposite sex.

I was also becoming more aware of politics. Greece is both an ancient and a new country. Since antiquity, it has been invaded, occupied and divided, becoming a single independent country again only in 1830. Cyprus remained part of the Ottoman Empire until 1878 when it came under the control of the United Kingdom. The two major population groups, Greek and Turkish, had co-existed uneasily until I was in my early teens when the Cyprus Emergency began.

The relationship between the Greeks and Turks has alternated between mutual hostility and reconciliation ever since Greece's independence in 1821. There have been various wars between the two countries since then with an exchange of large populations in Asia Minor (1914-1922) in the Western part of Turkey and the expulsion of Greeks from Constantinople (now known as Istanbul) in 1955. The Turks have been a thorn in the side of the Greeks for many centuries.

It wasn't until I was at the gymnasium that the relevance of all of this became apparent to me. When we visited Auntie Irene, we would sometimes veer off up to the top of Lapithos into the village. Chrysoula would say, 'This is a Turkish school,' and I would acknowledge that it was tiny compared to ours in Karavas or to the gymnasium for older students. It had steps leading up to it and a cement front area with a door leading to a one room school.

When I was little, the Greek Cypriots always thought they were superior to the Turks but I had no comprehension of what this would lead to. We lived in Paradise and had no reason to ever believe that would change. Once when I was going by bus to Nicosia, I saw these rundown little bothies made out of mud. I remember asking who lived there.

'They are Turkish houses,' I was told.

All I remember thinking is, *not good*, and knowing that, as a people, we didn't consort with them, but I wasn't actually aware of many Turkish people in my world. My Auntie Irene employed a Turkish man on her subsistence farm, but I had no personal contact or experience of them. I would have felt scared had I faced any Turks as we had been indoctrinated by the belief that they were a different breed, and the enemy of the Greeks.

This culture had been part of my life as far back as I can remember. Mother would say, 'We don't have Turks living in Karavas because we are protected by St Mary at the monastery.' There was a sense that we needed protection by the church and that there was something dangerously different about them, something worrying and dark.

My father had a couple of Turkish men working for him in his business in Kyrenia and there was a peasant who came to Karavas to buy bananas, but we children had no contact of which I was aware. I soon started realising that there were Turks and there were Greeks, and that we had nothing to do with each other. We had different customs, cultures and religions and were suspicious of each other, not without cause as it would transpire.

My school was a breeding ground for nationalism – *Enosis* (the political union of Cyprus and Greece, as an aim or ideal of certain Greeks and Cypriots) was always in the background. My mother's family, through my pappous, was very closely connected to the Greeks from the mainland. Many other families had only tenuous links with the mainland and for generations had lived in Cyprus. We all spoke the Greek language however, the Cypriot dialect is reputed to be closer, purer, to the original Greek language than the rest of the dialects of Greece. As students we desperately tried to emulate the Athenians. During the National holidays, the 28th October and 25th March, we would all assemble in front of the school and listen for hours to speech after speech. On one of these occasions, on a very hot day and after standing for some time, to my great embarrassment I fainted.

When Chrysoula went to the gymnasium, she started going to the Pantheon which took place early in the morning on the National Greek holiday of 25th March which celebrated Greece became free from the Turkish occupation. It was a widely celebrated day, a national holiday both in Greece and Cyprus although Cyprus had a different history. Cyprus had been bought from the Turks and became a British protectorate in 1878 and eventually a British Crown colony until its independence on 19th February 1959.

Yet another national holiday for Greece was 28th October which saw the end of the Nazi occupation in Greece and the islands (1941-45), celebrated with fervour both in Greece and Cyprus. The Germans had really ill-treated the Greeks, they created havoc and burned many of the villages during the war.

The events of 25th March were very exciting to me as a child. There was a big parade from the gymnasium and the pupils would all get up at the crack of dawn and dress in their best, perfectly ironed uniforms. Ever since my sister Chrysoula went to Lapithos Gymnasium, I had watched with envy as she prepared for the parade. There was a great deal of excitement in the house waiting to hear the drums, the trumpets and the patriotic songs as they passed down the main road of Karavas, with the sixth formers proudly leading the way.

When I took part, only once before everything changed, I felt simultaneously excited and frightened. It was so early as we walked up the steep roads in Lapithos with only the sound of dogs barking. There was not a soul to be seen anywhere, except the occasional stray cat darting across the street. Once we had assembled, loudly and enthusiastically singing patriotic songs, we would course through the Turkish communities where people made sure all their shutters were tightly closed. We were safe and confident in our large group and It never occurred to me how offensive this was to the people whose streets we paraded through and that they might be as frightened as I had been. It was both exciting and frightening, my heart was beating so loudly as I looked around me for anything unexpected happening but desperately hoping nothing would arise.

This was my first and last time joining the parade. When the EOKA troubles started, it became far too dangerous to have such events through Turkish communities. The Turks (who at the time made up 18% of the population) started to stir as the EOKA guerrilla organisation began their efforts to achieve independence from the UK and potential union with Greece. EOKA was led by Georgios Grivas, a Greek army officer and veteran of both World Wars I and II. Gregoris Afxentiou was recruited shortly after as team leader. The movement against colonialism was strong in the 1950s. The Empire was crumbling in countries such India, Egypt, Burma and Ceylon all of which wanted their independence. Britain had survived the war but its wealth, prestige and authority was very much reduced. Cyprus was important to them and to their US allies, because of its strategic position. The same could be said of all the receding occupiers: the Egyptians, the Romans, the Venetians and the Ottoman Empire all understood the strategic value of Cyprus. Empires are ruthless, particularly when threatened, and the treatment of Cyprus by the UK government had led to massive resentment. They used the classic tactic of divide and rule, encouraging Turkish Cypriots to oppose EOKA and the Movement of ENOSIS union with Greece. This culminated in the invasion of the island in 1974. Many people lost their lives and the result was the partition of Cyprus up to this day. The Turks ended up occupying disproportionately large part of Cyprus but I am running ahead of myself with the story here.

The EOKA organisation was equally ruthless. They targeted the youngsters at school and instilled importance and purpose in them. But perhaps this was the only way to fight such an unequal war, a war with Britain and Empire after all. The situation deteriorated rapidly and soon there were no rules or moral order to follow. Quite often, people with a grudge would get rid of someone in the name of EOKA and would spread rumours about them, saying that they were in collaboration with the enemy and therefore traitors.

One of my uncle's favourite stories, which he often repeated, was that he was taken prisoner during WWII and transported to Italy where they were fed on horse meat. I was horrified by this but had never thought such things, such threats of war and the fears attached to it, would ever come into my world. He said that he was on the firing line but managed to escape as a young Italian woman pulled him away at the last moment and a few moments later he heard the shooting. My uncle was very close to my mother and she took care of him up until he married. I have a feeling that my father may have been a little resentful of my mother and uncle's relationship. Stories like this were evidence that war had played a large part in the history of my family, but it was not until I was at the gymnasium that I really felt it in my own life too. Political strife was increasing and there was an air of fear surrounding us all.

I was twelve years old when my youngest brother, Sotiris, was born and I must admit that, with the self-absorption of youth, I had started getting weary of my mother's numerous pregnancies. Sotiris was her sixth surviving child, Thomas and Nicolas had died in infancy and she had suffered two miscarriages. There was no reliable form of contraception in those days and big families were the norm. It was not unusual to have twelve children in a family and I wonder how many Mama would have had if the children had all survived. Sadly, Sotiris was born with a learning disability. He only started to crawl at the age of three and took some uncertain steps when he was four. He remained without speech throughout his short life. Sotiris had pneumonia when aged twenty months but, unlike Thomas and Nicolas, he survived it thanks to oxygen cylinders brought all the way from Nicosia. Like his cousin, Pambos, and probably Nicolas and Thomas, he was probably afflicted by ATRX syndrome. Our entire family loved our little brother and our parents never hid him away as had happened to cousin Pambos. She always included Sotiris and treated him just like her other children: in many ways she favoured him.

So many changes were happening, both within and out with our family. My father's position became very difficult as politics became more intense. His background, his upbringing, his whole way of life was British, and his main business was absolutely dependent on people from Britain. Many of his regular clients were, high profile British politicians. This was not safe; this was not something which was going by unnoticed.

Mr Lennox Boyd, the Minister of External Affairs at the time, was a friend of his. Papa had his picture on the wall in his office, and at home we had a picture of his family as we had got to know them well. Lady French, Papa's alleged British mistress, would often visit the family in Karavas and we returned the visits now and again. Lady French was a very good artist and Father often accompanied her on her various painting excursions. I believe some of Lady French's paintings are permanent exhibits in the Visual Arts Gallery in Nicosia. She used to live with a full time housekeeper just above the Kyrenia Harbour with amazing views. I enjoyed visiting her there with my sister, and that's when I was first initiated to English high teas. It is odd to think that we had such a comfortable relationship with the woman who was said to be having a relationship with my father, and even Mother would be perfectly welcoming to her, but that is just how it was. Our closeness to her, though, would not have gone unmarked.

Papa was proud to be associated with these people and others like them. He could speak their language well and knew their way of life. He was comfortable in their company but unfortunately, the local people were resentful of him. His competitors wanted him out of the way and there were many threats made. He didn't take it seriously.

'School kid threats, Maro,' he said to me once. 'Nothing more than school kid threats.' I suppose they were to some extent but there was always an underlying worry that they were supported by sinister people in the background. Papa carried on as before; he was not doing any harm, his conscience was clear and he said that he felt safe, even when his car was being tampered with.

Terrifyingly, the situation became worse. British soldiers could be seen everywhere, students were throwing stones at the jeeps full of soldiers, there was general rebellion and unrest everywhere. It was during this time that an order came from the colonial government that all teachers at the gymnasium from mainland Greece should return to Greece. Lapithos gymnasium became depleted and, there was practically no one left to teach us. A group of students including myself and my sister were sent to the Kyrenia gymnasium by their parents. The situation was serious, we were all caught up in the politics of the day. However, it was not as straightforward as that – we were certainly not welcomed by the students at the Kyrenia gymnasium. They were openly hostile and I couldn't make friends with anyone, they literally turned their backs on us. It was devastating for me, especially when I had been so comfortable and confident and knew everyone at the Lapithos gymnasium. One by one, the students who had originally left the Lapithos school for the Kyrenia gymnasium returned back to Lapithos but Mama was adamant we stayed there – our education was paramount to her and we had to stay whether we liked it or not. I was very unhappy. I stopped functioning intellectually, my learning capacity dropped to a minimum. From being on top of the class, I was now hovering at the bottom. It was a horrible feeling after experiencing so much success which I had assumed to be my birthright.

The worst was yet to come ...

Gymnasium

Chapter Eleven

I t was the 30th of January 1957.

Not a special date when you write it on a piece of paper, but one which would turn our lives upside down and mark us all forever.

It must have been about 8pm and I was busy at my writing desk in front of the window doing my homework for the next day. It was dark outside, as it had been all day, the wind howling, the rain splattering on the windowpanes. There seemed to be rattling noises everywhere. The rain can be torrential in Karavas during winter, the wind howls with all its might and the rain pours in seemingly never-ending sheets. On that night, apart from the weather, the house was still and quiet.

Chrysoula was also studying in her bedroom, and my four younger siblings were fast asleep in their beds. I would have hated to be out in that weather and I thought of how privileged we all were to be safely indoors, unlike other poor souls who were no doubt trying to fruitlessly find shelter. I could not relax despite being safe indoors. Papa wasn't home from work yet. This wasn't unusual in itself; he was a diligent man and it was always hard to predict when he would return. Despite knowing this, there was a niggle of worry inside me, something which made it impossible to settle.

Suddenly, there was a loud knocking on the large wooden front door. *Who could that be at this time of night?*, I wondered. In the middle of the storm, I heard my mother's footsteps going towards the door. There was the noise of the large bolt being pulled back and the door opened. A man's gruff voice was heard but I couldn't make out what he was saying, the wind was too loud, and I was too far away. A moment later, I heard the voice of a second man, but still the words were no more than a mumble to me.

I moved slowly towards the door, trying to make out what was being said when, all of a sudden, I heard Mama screaming and howling, the most terrible noise, like an animal in pain. I rushed out to the hall and saw her in a terrible state, her hands at her face, wailing in agony. I could hardly make out what she was saying, she was incoherent. The men had gone, the front door was closed, there was only my mother and the unholy noise coming from her.

'Mama! What is wrong, what is wrong?' I asked her.

She raised her eyes to me as if she couldn't quite work out who I was or why I was standing there. 'Mama?' I asked again. 'Mama, what is wrong?'

'They killed him, Maro – they killed him!' she wept.

'What are you talking about? Who has been killed?' I demanded.

'Your father! Your father has been killed!'

The story seeped though both agonisingly slowly as the reality of what she was saying hit me, but also sickeningly swift in its brutality. Between her words, the men at the door who must have been police, and the terrible words I pieced together, there was a horrible finality to what had occurred. I crumpled on the sofa next to Mama, my body instantly weak as I placed my arm around her shoulder feeling my own body sway with her sobs.

Father had been shot dead.

Murdered.

The noise had brought Chrysoula, Despo and Andreas into the hall and they too tried to work out what had happened. The words were too cruel, too vicious, but all of us had to face up to them.

The story unfolded, although there was not much of it. Papa had been in the restaurant next to his office at 2pm having lunch. He went there every day, a creature of habit whose movements would have been easy to predict. There were no other diners there as two masked men ran in and shot him stone dead. The proprietor claimed he only heard shots but saw nothing.

A man of only 42 years old.

A man with a wife.

A man with six children ranging from sixteen years of age to only two.

Just another story in a newspaper, but a story which had so much behind the headline. I was only fourteen and this would change my life forever.

The large hall with the arch in the middle, was normally the hub of the family, but now it was the scene of horror. So many times, we had been there having fun, it was the place where I danced to the gramophone but now it would become a mortuary for my father.

I could hear my mother say, 'Monsieur Dupre! Let us get Monsieur Dupre!' over and over. She was delirious and ranting about a French surgeon who lived nearby.

'What good would that do?' I asked her.

'Monsieur Dupre! He will bring Kypros back to life!' she wept. 'We must get the surgeon; he will bring him back – someone must go for him now before it is too late.'

'It *is* too late. Papa has gone. There is not a surgeon in the world who can breathe life into him now,' I said.

'But a new heart perhaps? He could put a new heart in him?'

She was desperate. Despite my young years I knew that the situation was hopeless, there couldn't be another Lazarus. Jesus Christ wouldn't perform another miracle. There was nothing we could do or say to bring her to her senses. Eventually, we retired to bed, but sleep wouldn't come that night or for many nights to come.

Early next morning, we gathered in the kitchen and I recalled the scene of only twenty-four hours earlier. All of us had been there which was an unusual situation at that period in our lives. Papa had been drinking his tea and eating a slice of Mama's fruitcake. Thea had been on his lap, her fair skin and blonde hair the same as his, reflected in his love, the apple of his eye. Despo had been looking on with a slightly envious air, while Mama sat with my toddler brother Sotiris on her lap, Andreas next to her and my sister Chrysoula on my right. It was a beautiful family picture and it had been shattered forever. Had that been our final farewell? Somehow, had we been blessed with that moment which would stay in our minds forever?

As I pondered, I realised that the feelings of nervousness and anxiety I had been experiencing had gone. Papa had been targeted in many small ways for some time, but now the ultimate act of violence had occurred. Did I no longer have anything to fear? This had to be the work of EOKA. Papa had always said that the actions we had seen were just those of schoolchildren, but I had never believed that – sadly, I had been correct. I firmly believed that Papa had been seen as too close to the British and he had paid the ultimate price.

That morning, we travelled to the mortuary in Kyrenia, one of my Papa's chauffeurs giving us a lift in Papa's green Chevrolet which had been his pride and joy. We were to collect the coffin and body from the mortuary to bring it home to Karavas. The coffin was eventually secured, and we travelled the eight miles or so home. The journey seemed to last forever and was a terrible ordeal. I remember getting into the back of the car wishing it was all over, but the burial was still to come.

The coffin with my dead father was put at the end of our large hall for the funeral the next day. It was a place where I had danced to my first gramophone record, where the family had sat together, where I had fun with my siblings. Now it was silent and would always have an air of grief.

It seemed like hundreds of people invaded our house the following morning, the day of the funeral. The news of my father's murder had spread like wildfire. People could hardly believe it, many of them weeping inconsolably. Mama had to be strong for them, but when some of our own family arrived, she could no longer keep up such a brave face and needed their support.

We went to the cemetery near the foot of the mountain about a mile outside the village. The procession of the funeral was followed by thousands of people. All the inhabitants of Karavas and the adjacent villages were there either because they loved him or envied him or out of curiosity. I could barely process the service and hated seeing the earth covering my father's body. Eventually it was all over and we were home again. I can't remember anything else happening that day apart from the burial. Maybe I have blocked it out. What could possibly have been gained from this murder? How could the nationalists (assuming it was them) believe that this would further their cause? That the death of one man, a husband and father of six, would make their political hopes come true was ludicrous – all they had done was senseless and cruel.

I do remember the meagre meal my mother attempted to cook that evening – a type of potato ragout. My siblings and mother and I sat around the table, my father's space at the head of the table remaining empty as it always would from this day forward. I looked at my meal but not a single bite was taken. In fact, I could never face that dish ever again, the association has been too bitter to bear.

On the next day, I happened to pass by the wide opened garage door of our house. My father's favourite green Chevrolet was inside and just at the entrance on the right-hand side corner I saw a large tin tub in which mother used to bathe us as babies, full to the top with red, bloody water. My father's beautifully tailored smoky blue suit, the one he was wearing when murdered, full of bullet holes, was soaking in the water.

My mother appeared to be functioning well after the first few days that followed the funeral and there was no repetition of her cries for Monsieur Dupre, but soon the realisation hit her. Kypros was dead. A form of breakdown crept in. She had never been poetic or musical, but she started composing songs about the situation and singing in a mournful voice. I found myself in a hopeless situation – it seemed as if my mother was going mad, I had lost my father, and there was nothing I could do to remedy either fact. After a little while, Mama did manage to pull herself together – she was an intelligent, resourceful woman and despite all her misery and the tragedy we now faced, she forced herself to assume responsibility for her six children.

Every day, with Chrysoula, I would walk the two or so miles to the cemetery to visit my father's grave. We were young and fit, there was no problem walking there, but it felt heavy, as if something was oppressing us. There was nothing good left in the world, I felt, there was only evil. Sometimes Mother and our other siblings would come, sometimes not. We had a car in the garage but nobody could drive it: women didn't drive in those days.

In a matter of days, Chrysoula and I transformed my father's grave into a beautiful little garden. One day, late in the afternoon as the sun dipped below the horizon, we headed as usual to the cemetery. I noticed from afar that something untoward was going on near the grave. It transpired that a group of teenage boys were busy uprooting the plants which we so carefully planted and throwing them here and there. I was very angry and shouted at them as they ran away. They ran as fast as they could towards the mountain as I chased after them, my anger swelling and the adrenaline pushing me on. I kept running after them, not really thinking what would have happen if I caught them. At least I would have taught them a lesson, those ignorant empty-headed children. Mother was pleased that the little ruffians had been run out of sight but of course angry about the incident. It brought home to us all the general lack of respect and empathy in our society.

Until we were forced to move schools, I was daring, confident and popular and had many friends. I was excelling both academically and in sport. I was good looking and had everything a young person could ever want. The colonial government stole my confidence when they essentially closed my school but the nationalists stole my father and ended my childhood.

When my father was murdered, not only did I have to process the trauma, but the increasing violence of the political situation had hit home in the most awful way and I could see it throughout our country. My lines of thinking became so different that I couldn't really function, and things tumbled down. I couldn't concentrate on my studies anymore and from my place at the top of the class, I soon hovered at the bottom.

What I learned during those times was just how randomly cruel life could be. One day I hit a low – my test results were awful and so was everything else. My school life in Kyrenia was not getting any better, on the contrary it was getting worse. Mother had become a recluse; she wouldn't even go to visit her sister Ophelia. Some neighbours continued to come into the house for something to eat and a chat. Both Uncle Panayiotis and Uncle Alexander would pass by on their way to the shops further up the village, but those were the only people with whom she had contact. It was still winter, there wasn't much work to be done in the fields, there were only the animals to attend to and she had nothing to distract her from her loss.

I was desolate and really wanted to end it all.

Growing in hedgerows on our land were death camas lilies. They thrived like thistles, not dangerous to the touch but impossible to eat. The leaves were tough and spiky, rather like a cactus. Hidden within the stem lay a deadly poison which we had always been warned about as children. Even if only a little was taken, death would soon follow. I had always, naturally, avoided the plant but now I was curious. Could it be the answer to my feelings of loss and despair? Did I want to find out just how powerful it could be?

I only swallowed a little of the poison, but it was enough for me to feel terrible symptoms within an hour. I was soon doubled up in agony with stomach pains and desperately wished I had never chosen to take this option. I ran back to the house so that I could go to the toilet, but Mama saw that I was ill, and I knew that I couldn't tell her what I had done. Her heart was already broken, she didn't need to know that her daughter wished for life to be over. As a young child, I had suffered from dysentery and, luckily, she believed I was suffering from another episode. I was put to bed for two days in agony. I had appalling diarrhoea and broke out in a horrific, angry rash. I eventually regained my health but never spoke the truth to Mama. I had now dabbled with darkness myself and realised that life was something I wanted to cling onto, not escape.

Chapter Twelve

Mama basically became a recluse. She wouldn't leave home to see her sister, she would only see my uncles passing through the house now and again. We all prayed that she would come out of this state and, in time, she did. It took a little while, but she gradually recovered sufficiently to come to a very important decision.

Chrysoula and I were to leave Karavas and continue our studies in England. It would have been my father's wish; in fact, we spoke about it well before his death when he took such pleasure and pride in associating with high society British people. After all these were the people who saved him, and he would wish that his daughters would also enjoy that life. These people had pulled him out of the streets, out of poverty and hunger and given him shelter from the storms. They had taught him the English language (my father was a well-spoken person and spoke English without an accent) and good manners. They had made him the person he was, and he was not to know that would also be his downfall. I was proud to have had him as my father despite his flaws and I was happy to continue with his wishes even if it meant leaving my home. In less than a couple of months all would be over with Karavas and I was excited at the prospect of new beginnings, a new life and adventure.

After my initial excitement it is true that I had a few misgivings about leaving my mother and siblings. Mama said that as we were the eldest, further education had to be sorted for us immediately, whereas the others still had time. There was a big, interesting wide world out there to explore, the world was our oyster and we had to reach for the stars. I knew this was true, but it was still a big step, especially after such turmoil with Father's murder. Lady French paid us a visit on a number of occasions after the murder, but I have no idea how she was feeling. I can only speculate. She must have been missing Father a great deal. Some of it would be guilt I would imagine as it was his friendship with these people that had made Father a target for the nationalists.

Those who had shot him had used political differences as an excuse for murder and had rid themselves of a competitor or a man of whom they were jealous. My father was not the only victim of the times. There were other families who were left bereft and impoverished, their children merely existing for years to come. At least we were fortunate in that we had the means to survive.

It was about six weeks between being told we would go to England and actually leaving in July. We could take one old-fashioned trunk with us, to share, with all of our clothes and everything we needed. I took some photographs which I have carried with me over the years, but I had no other special things. I was looking forward to it and was positive about it all, my new, challenging, exciting life. You would think I would be quite frightened but I wasn't. Lady French came to see my mother and said she would do everything she could to help. She gave Mama lots of advice about life in Britain and how young people should behave. My hair was very long and she suggested to have it cut so it would be nice and neat for my new school.

'It cannot be straggly just because you like it that way,' she told me, firmly. 'I will be taking you to the Ritz when I am in London and it is important that you look tidy.' I had no resentment towards Lady French. She did her best and I cannot judge what happened between her and my father. We assumed that they had been lovers but had no evidence nor did anyone speak of it. I think that she wanted to maintain an association with us because of Papa and she may also have felt some small degree of guilt that the British link had brought about his death.

No one told me how to look after myself in other ways, whether fiscally, emotionally or sexually. All of that was ignored. I was very naïve and self-absorbed and didn't even know what Chrysoula was feeling nor did I think to ask. Everything about our new life was decided by the higher echelons who knew our family, with Lady French at the head of it all. Mama just followed their advice. At that time, the culture between England and Cyprus was like night and day. She wouldn't have been able to comprehend anyway what it would be like for me and my sister to go into that environment. No matter how clever she was, she could not see beyond her immediate experience – nor even beyond her village to be honest. She was in the dark, just like us. We all took every part of the situation as we found it and accepted it as it was. Chrysoula and I knew that we were going to live with a lady in her own home rather than a boarding school, the reason being that we would learn much more about the culture that way. Lady French tried to be helpful with the arrangements and we greatly appreciated that help since she had a better idea than we did of what faced us. England seemed so far away and very different. Chrysoula and I would leave Cyprus at the end of our school year at the Kyrenia gymnasium.

One day, I had just finished my lessons and was walking down to catch my rickety old bus for home. I was feeling hot and clammy but I couldn't follow the shorter route as there was a group of girls walking that way and I didn't want to join them. Still, I had plenty of time so I turned to the left. As I walked, I thought of the Bishop of Kyrenia, a big obese man with piercing small blue eyes and a reputation for being a womaniser, dressed in his silk cape with his big pectoral cross and ecclesiastical ring standing at the pulpit some time ago and preaching to an overflowing congregation about Enosis, a political speech he presented with buckets of sweat coming off him. His strong, resonant voice was still ringing in my ears. *The imperialists, the capitalists*, he kept saying, as the sweat poured.

I continued on my way to the little bus station – there were very few people about, most of the locals were probably having their siestas. I stood on the steps waiting for my bus to arrive and looked across the road to where my father's office next to the restaurant stood empty and forlorn, all boarded up. A shiver went down my spine and I could hardly step onto the bus. Things had changed so much, so quickly and there were more changes to come. Soon I wouldn't leave my school for home, these bus journeys would be just a memory, I would reflect on things such as the politics of my homeland and fat bishops preaching about politics without living them. A new life was waiting for me. it was time to go and I felt fine about that.

The last few weeks in Cyprus went by in a flash. It seemed as if the day of our departure arrived almost without any warning. The only thing I remember is the open-air café at Famagusta where we waited until it was time to embark on the boat to Italy, from where we would travel across Europe by train to Calais. Maybe we arrived far too early but it felt like we were there forever, waiting for the next chapter of our lives to begin. Mama and Auntie Irene were there and it felt as if we were all just waiting for something to happen – which, eventually, it did. I think that my subconscious has blocked some memories of that day as I remember only bits of it, as if a film is jumping between scenes. I don't even remember the last goodbye to Mama and Auntie.

From the café, the next thing I recall is being on the boat and things feeling surreal. I had only ever been on a boat once before, when I was ten or eleven and Papa had taken us to visit a naval ship at Kyrenia which was open to visitors. I enjoyed the visit immensely especially when a young officer dressed in his white uniform who was showing us around lifted me up to help me down from the top of the stairs. I thought him so handsome at the time! This, however, was a very different state of affairs.

People were generally helpful and friendly on the boat - because of the EOKA troubles, a lot of travellers were emigrating to other parts of the world and a significant number of them to the UK. We were all in a very similar situation. A little group of three or four young men attached themselves to us and we found it difficult to shake them off. It was absolutely fine whilst we were on the boat where there

On the boat to England with my sister Chrysoula

125

was plenty of room to move around, but pretty unpleasant when we boarded the train to go through Europe. An eighteen-year-old sat next to me in the railway carriage and I was horrified when he started to fondle me overnight when everybody was asleep, and the carriage was in darkness. I was too young, naïve and inexperienced to know how to deal with the situation. Just when I thought the nightmare of the railway journey was over, there was more to come.

I cannot recall how we eventually arrived at Dover or even catching the train to London Victoria, everything is so blurred. I had never seen so many people bundled together in such a confined space, not even during National Greek celebrations. People were pushing, shoving, shouting and rushing about. All I could think was that I needed to stay next to my sister at all costs. The idea of getting separated with no English language on my side and not knowing where I was going was very scary. I had the impression that Chrysoula was given some instructions before we left and as she had a better command of English, I was happy to let her lead the way. Glancing at her, I realised that she was equally worried and frightened about the situation.

'I don't know what to do either, Maro – but I will find out.'

In a flash, she disappeared and left me petrified. I decided that the best things to do was to remain pinned to the floor, hoping that she would remember where she had left me. I was pushed here and there by the crowd but tried not to move. For many years, up until recently that has stayed with me as a recurrent nightmare – I have been haunted by being stranded in a city, thoroughly lost and trying to find something or someone familiar without having any success, a repetition of my first time at Victoria Station.

Under normal circumstances, I should have had a better knowledge of the English language after three years at the gymnasium but education had been so disrupted for us and now I was paying the price. Chrysoula was a couple of years older and had a slightly better command of it. After a few minutes - which seemed like a lifetime - she reappeared along with a strange woman.

'This is Mrs Morley,' said my sister. 'She will help us.'

No introductions were made by Mrs Morley herself but it turned out that she was supposed to have been our social worker in England. We followed her to her parked car outside the station. Although June, it was dark, drizzly and quite chilly. I thought to myself, *I don't really like it here, I want to go home* and I would have done if I could. We drove for a long time, heading for Surrey and the small village of Ashtead, to Oakfield Road and a house called The Oak Trees. This was to become my home for the next three years. I had no idea at the time what was happening.

The Oak Trees was a large Victorian house on three floors with a sizeable front and back garden. It was owned by a lady called Mrs Jones who was to be our foster mother while we were in England, at least for the foreseeable future. We arrived there late in the evening and were taken straight to our room on the second floor, a large spacious room with three single beds. The two at the far end were for us and the one at the other end was for Susan, the eldest of Mrs Jones' three daughters. Exhausted from the journey we quickly got ready for bed and were fast asleep within minutes. Mrs Morley disappeared as I can't even remember saying goodbye to her and she didn't even check where we were to sleep. Her visits were rare and of no value, her checks on our welfare non-existent. She was aloof, always beautifully dressed in a blue suit, tall and slim, with short, permed hair and never without her high heeled stilettos – she appeared to have a complete lack of interest in me and my sister.

On the morning after our arrival, I woke up hearing this funny noise under my bay window. *Clop clop clop* it went, and I could only assume it was someone on horseback. It was much later I realised it was actually some young woman running in her heels, down the road to catch her bus! I got up eventually and dressed very slowly, but the realisation of where we were hit me and I couldn't move. This was it, this was my life now, and it did not feel like something to enjoy or anything like I had envisaged. I fell on the pillow, my tears soaking through the thin fabric. I decided that I must be unwell to feel like this, there was something terribly wrong with me. Looking back, I was really just homesick. Chrysoula was not there, she had already gone downstairs - I was alone in this strange room, this strange place, with feelings I couldn't understand.

I went downstairs. The house was empty and quiet. Mrs Jones was at the far end of the garden and I realised I hadn't really taken her in the night before. She was a slim, attractive woman in her early 40s, her hair was nicely styled with large curls, slightly purple in colour and she clearly looked after herself. I hoped that she would be kind and that I would soon feel settled. I stood at the back door and looked around me. I saw a long, tidy flower garden with a rockery at the right-hand side. Beyond that, there was a little hedge with a gate in the middle leading to the vegetable garden. Mrs Jones was working in the little vegetable patch in the right-hand corner. I headed towards her and she smiled when she saw me.

'Good morning – did you have a good sleep?' she asked.

I spotted a swing and moved towards it and sat down.

'Yes, thank you,' I replied, always remembering my manners even if I felt rather empty inside. I remained on the swing watching her doing a little gardening and after a few minutes she turned back to me again.

'Would you like some coffee?' she enquired. I nodded. 'And do you take sugar?'

I didn't really understand her question and, despite the fact that I did take sugar, replied, 'No thank you.' The coffee duly arrived, sugarless. I was so much looking forward to drinking it, but I could only take a few sips and poured the rest away while she wasn't looking. I worked on my dislike however and since that time, stopped taking sugar in my tea and coffee, largely because Mrs Jones would always say to people, 'She doesn't like sugar.'

'I think people in this country will have difficulty pronouncing your name,' she told me later that day. 'I'm not terribly sure how to do it myself. Let's call you Mary. That will do.'

And with that, she took my name of Maro from me.

I soon discovered that Mrs Jones was a bitter, twisted lady and probably because I was not very interactive due to the barrier of my lack of English, she more or less froze me out. She was protective over her own children making sure they were not feeling less fortunate financially than the rest of us. She was given money to look after us and would send any surplus left back home to my mother saying that her expenditure was less than she had expected. This was odd because she was always pleading poverty up to the extent of buying secondhand blazers, tennis rackets and other clothing for us when school opened because she couldn't buy new clothes for her children. She didn't want them to feel underprivileged compared to us.

Her eldest daughter Susan was my own age, she was a big girl, broad and tall, more mature and older looking than me. She wasn't particularly kind or pleasant to my sister when school started, and they were put in the same year. Gwen (a

Welsh name as Mrs Jones was Welsh), the middle girl, was my favourite. She was intelligent and pleasant looking, always helpful and talkative. She was the only normal person in the family! The youngest, Mary, was nearly four years of age and wasn't a particularly likeable child. She was extremely spoiled and because she was thought to be overweight, was always on a diet. Her mother monitored her food intake very carefully. In fact, everything was carefully measured by Mrs Jones and the portions were always controlled for all of us. I suppose it must have been very difficult to afford so many people living in the house but there was definitely money coming in to look after me and my sister.

I was very unhappy with Mrs Jones. She was stiff and indifferent towards me for the full three years I was there. She never warmed to me; she never became a second mother. She was a bitter woman who felt sorry for herself and I always thought she felt that she deserved a better life. She came from an upper middle-class family and was so particular about manners and keeping to rules – put the spoon in the right place she would say, never put your hands on the table beyond your elbows, cut the toast in a particular way, take a bite and put it down, don't hold it in the air! We had to be spotlessly clean with pristine uniforms, food was very restricted, and it was unheard of to simply help oneself to something to eat. It was not like a home to us. Sometimes, if I was studying late which often happened, I would sneak to the larder after midnight and get a slice of white bread with butter and Marmite. It tasted so good, but it was a military operation to ensure that Mrs Jones wouldn't sniff out any signs of my misbehaviour! Every crumb had to be wiped up, the knife cleaned, and all evidence removed. The food was very different to that at home, but I did enjoy it. I particularly enjoyed the food at school, the buns with pink and white icing which were provided during our morning break and all of the stodgy food I had never been brought up with did appeal to me. I actually put on a stone after coming to Britain and was shocked when I was weighed at school one day!

There were two other girls boarding at the house. One of them, Daisy, was a big girl, tall and broad and slightly bigger than Susan. Daphne was a very intelligent girl, very friendly with Susan who really looked up to her. The other girl, Betty, was not as intelligent and she didn't achieve entrance to Sutton Public Day School Trust (GPDST) where the others went and where Chrysoula and I planned to go. Betty was a skinny, pale obnoxious girl, maybe a year older than me. She studied politics at school and was often discussing the Cyprus situation with Mrs Jones whilst she was preparing our high tea in the evenings. She used to annoy me immensely with her views and she favoured the Turks of course. It seemed as if I was surrounded by people who thought they knew better than me and I could only wait for the day when I would come into my own once more.

Chapter Thirteen

In July after our arrival, my sister and I attended the World Girl Guide Jamboree at Windsor Great Park. This was to mark the centenary of the birth of Lord Baden Powell. It was a fantastic experience meeting girls from across the world with everyone friendly and delighted to be there. The highlight was the visit from the Queen to our unit. I still have the photos from her visit in my album! It made me feel a little happier to be in England and I started to look forward to the next stage of my life.

September soon came and with that, we began our studies at the Sutton Day School Trust (GPDST). Dressed in our purple summer school uniform and straw hat with a ribbon around it, we walked through the Ashtead Commons to the railway station to catch the train for Sutton. Once there, we had to walk for another mile or so to school every morning. I was full of excitement but also trepidation about what was to come that first day. New school, new people, new friends – and I was doing it all with very little English. The girls who already attended the school were clearly happy to be back, there was lots of laughter, and I got some friendly smiles and a 'hello' from a few of them but they soon realised that I couldn't really speak English.

They were pleasant girls and helpful – gradually, as my language and confidence improved, I made more and more friends. I certainly made the effort and they responded well towards me. Just like me, they were privileged to be attending such a good school. It was a Girls Day Trust School (Greater London) established in 1884 and still always on, I believe, the Sunday Times Top 100 Independent schools list in the UK. The building was old, full of corridors, with classrooms of all sizes and so many outbuildings it was like a maze. There were many tennis courts and sports fields, including a cricket green. The school was crazy about sport. The first thing which surprised me was the food. I was quite amazed to have a cold half pint of milk and a bun with white icing on top (sometimes pink!) during my first morning break. Lunches were delicious and, I loved the desserts – treacle pudding, syrup pudding, tarts and sponges. The type of food I would have now and again became the norm. I soon put on weight, but only temporarily.

After my traumatic experiences in Cyprus and with practically no schooling during the last two years, I had started Sutton High School afresh with any pre-existing learning completely wiped out. I was a complete novice, even the language was new. I pressed on however and the school was excellent and I enjoyed my three years there a great deal.

The teachers at Sutton Grammar were selected very carefully, only ever from the top universities. They were all very interested in my progress and even during lunchtime they would give me extra tuition. Miss Charlesworth was headmistress at the time, an exceptional woman who later worked with the United Nations. I particularly liked the teacher of Classics, Miss Wood, a tall Grecian looking lady with a good deportment and a very pleasant disposition. As time went on, she would often take our group to London to watch plays based on Ancient Greece and mythology. I remember once returning to catch the train to Sutton after being at the National Theatre to watch an Ancient Greek play. The train was packed and we had to remain standing. I was extremely tired after the evening's events and, without realising it, I said in a loud voice, 'Oh dear! I am so tired!' As a result, nearly everybody in the vicinity stood up to offer me their seat. My friends laughed and giggled about it to my embarrassment as I sat down!

On another occasion, Miss Wood's little bubble car was trapped by other vehicles and four bystanders lifted her car out and handed it over to her! She was very amused by the incident, in fact we all were! I loved the Science teacher's racing red MG which I would watch her parking in the yard below from the top school window. Perhaps my father's love of cars had rubbed off on me somewhat.

Miss Hammond, one of my English teachers, was tall and thin with short straight hair and a long fringe. She was serious and rather unapproachable, a classic old maid really. Between her attitude, my lack of English, and the naughtiness of my new friends, we both ended up in a rather awkward situation one day. With a great deal of prompting from my friends, I asked her to explain what 'necking' was – she was not amused!

Miss Bailey, my Religious Knowledge teacher was always strict and not very popular, but very good to me. I remember her saying, 'Poor Mary – it's all Greek to you.'

'I wish it was, Miss Bailey!' I replied, 'I wish it was.' She chuckled at that which was unusual!

Sutton High was a good school. Particular attention was paid to our school uniform and we were instructed in proper dress, correct deportment, and social skills. Trying to make us into ladies, as was the norm at that time. I enjoyed my English school years particularly as I made more and more friends who would often invite me to their homes for tea. One of my best friends was a girl called Janet Williams.

She would call me 'Beanie' and was forever preoccupied with drawing kidney bean shaped little people engaged in different activities. I was very amused by her imagination and talent. Janet was one of those gifted people who excelled at everything. Every Saturday we would both go to the Art School at Epsom until one of the art teachers got interested in me and Janet would tease me terribly about him. I thought of Janet many times throughout the years but, much to my regret, I never actively sought her out.

Mrs Jones had a male friend, a Dr Lesleywho worked at the Cottage Hospital in Leatherhead. Things went sour when Miss Gilmore, a nurse at the same hospital and a tenant of Mrs Jones living in the attic, became interested in him. He looked a bit like Bing Crosby I thought – unfortunately, he couldn't keep his hands off my breasts when sounding my chest and he wasn't a nice man at all.

I was now of the age when men were noticing me and I found that their attention was often most unwelcome. A driver who offered me a lift as I was walking back to Ashtead from Leatherhead after a visit to the dentist one day proceeded to masturbate while driving, asking me to assist him as the car was moving slowly. I opened the passenger door and said I would jump out if he didn't stop to let me out. I must have been rather naïve and trusting in those days. I learned quickly though and never accepted a lift again.

I quite fancied myself as an artist but I don't think I had much talent despite the fact I had decided to apply to Bath Art School once I left Sutton Grammar. I would go out sketching for hours, sometimes in remote places – I must have had a guardian angel keeping me safe considering there were so many predators about. Another form of escapism was the outdoor swimming pool on the outskirts of Ashtead. It was covered with water lilies, there were no sounds to be heard except those of nature. The water was deep and dangerous, and there was a sign saying *For Swimmers Only.* It took me back to happy days in Karavas.

There was no Mr Jones back at The Oaks and the reason became clear to me on our first Christmas there. Mrs Jones appeared rather agitated while we were waiting to be taken out for the day by Uncle Nicholas who was coming to take us to London to spend Christmas with him. It was then that Mrs Jones spoke to my sister and said that her family were invited to a friend's house and had to go soon. Would Chrysoula open the door to her ex-husband at 10am and tell him that the family was out? Chrysoula followed her instructions and a tall, slim man came to the door with tears streaming down his face when he was told he couldn't come in. He handed over a pile of Christmas gifts then left, leaving both of us upset too. Mrs Jones later told us she'd have to leave her husband due to the fact that his personality had changed having be traumatised by the war. It was probably the only time she opened up to us. In retrospect, her life must have been very difficult and having to take in lodgers to make ends meet would explain some of her evident resentment of us.

During the first two years with Mrs Jones, we had invitations from one or two of my father's old friends. One of the invitations came from The Right Honourable Alan Lennox Boyd, the Foreign Secretary who asked us to tea at his house. Mrs Jones' face was beaming. She tried to explain to us that this was a very special invitation and we should feel honoured. She made sure we were appropriately dressed on the day and soon we were knocking on his door at Eaton Place, near Downing Street. We just took the whole thing in our stride – we had been used to so many well-off people with Papa's business. The old Georgian building was very roomy, beautiful and impressive inside. I was particularly interested to see a big collection of walking sticks on the right-hand side as we entered the front door. They were curved with unusual tops, collected from all over the world. The lounge was massive, with unusual antique furniture and a deep piled carpet. The bathroom was very large and in it was the biggest Victorian bath I had ever seen. We had a very interesting and special afternoon and were looked after terribly well, even when the Minister had to leave for an important meeting. The last I heard of the Right Honourable Alan Lennox Boyd was close to my wedding when he sent me a gold fountain pen which I appreciated. It showed that he had never forgotten my family.

On several occasions we had invitations from Adrian and Rosemary Seligman who had been our tenants for a short time, Rosemary being the first to put the seed of physiotherapy in my mind. Rosemary and Adrian lived in Wimbledon. Their house was painted white and blue, and even the decoration inside was in Greek, Mediterranean colours and style. On one occasion we were taken to visit Adrian Seligman's parents. His mother, Hilda Seligman, was a writer. They had lived in India for a long time and she had written a book whilst there, 'When Peacocks Called'. She had given me a signed copy at the time, which I treasure. Adrian's father was a botanist and had an extensive collection of Alpine plants and flowers. We were taken on that day to The Savoy for our afternoon tea, where everything was so opulent. These moments were delightful and really took me back to a different life. They were snatches of indulgence far away from Mrs Jones' penny pinching and calorie counting.

Lady French also followed my progress, writing to me and later sending me a gift for my wedding. That was the last time I heard from her personally but she kept up with my life through my mother at home. Back then, she took us to

The Ritz for lunch (just as she had promised); there were so many courses, one after the other, I just couldn't face food afterwards! I suppose the situation with Lady French had always been unusual. Mother had perhaps known about her close relationship with my Father and accepted it. She had been in our lives for a long time and was involved in the preparations for sending us to England and kept in touch. It was both terribly civilised and also rather bizarre. I wonder what my mother truly felt about it all?

During our short school breaks at Easter and Christmas, we would go to Boscombe, near Bournemouth, to stay with Mrs Goodman, a lovely lady who became very dear to me. We had a lot of freedom and many happy times by the sea. During the long summer holidays, my mother would take us back home. The journey was longer through Europe by train and then on the boat through the Mediterranean, catching the boat from Venice. I used to love the journey home, but it was hard leaving again.

Uncle Nicolas took us to London on most weekends for lunch and to all the big musicals and shows at the time. Unfortunately, we had become rather spoiled and snobbish by then and used to take him for granted, which, looking back, I regret a great deal. Chrysoula and I had changed during our time in England, we had certainly moved on from being the young girls at one with nature and living in those golden moments of our upbringing. Perhaps we would always have become different people, but for me, the huge upheavals I had already experienced made me keen to achieve as much as possible. I wanted to be someone, I wanted to be acknowledged as a young woman who had gone far – I wanted recognition. I just didn't know how exactly I would go about it.

I had a boyfriend called Christopher at the time for two or three years during my stay in Surrey. His parents often invited me for tea at their beautiful home on the outskirts of Ashtead. His father was a banker in the City. We had met by chance at a dance at his school, Sutton Grammar School for Boys. We had good times together, we often went to Goodwood car races and it was especially exciting to watch Stirling Moss racing. Chris had a noisy motorbike which he would leave at the top of Oakfield Road for fear that Mrs Jones would complain. I did enjoy our time together often climbing Box Hill and Leith Hill and taking many walks around the area.

When I was still at Sutton High School in England, Costas – the boy from the other side of the river who used to push me on the Easter swing and always seemed to have a soft spot for me – came to find me at Mrs Jones' house. He arrived much to my surprise and her horror as I was with Christopher now. I did try to give some attention to Costas and we went out for the day but my heart was not in it. Costas came from a disadvantaged background and never managed to improve his situation. I believe he married an English girl, started a family early and never achieved material success, unlike some other Cypriots I knew.

Peter, the boy I had known since my school years in Cyprus when I used to talk to him over the wall, also visited me two or three times. He was perhaps a little disappointed I had changed in many ways: I was no longer the little girl he knew in Karavas.

'You are a rotten girl, Mary. You have them hanging on the string' Mrs Jones commented. I didn't like the comment one little bit but there was the possibility that she might have been right.

On my third and last Christmas in Surrey, when Chrysoula was at Liverpool University, she suggested that we should spend Christmas and New Year in Scotland. We stayed in a bed and breakfast in the affluent area of Corstorphine. It was bitterly cold but sunny, the frost was thick on the ground, and never before had I seen so many ladies wearing fur coats. I remember remarking to my sister that Edinburgh must be a very wealthy city and she agreed. I loved Edinburgh despite the cold. We joined in with all the New Year activities and had a tremendous time. I enjoyed my brief time in Scotland but could not ever have imagined it would become my home.

After that, it was back to the grindstone. Chrysoula went back to university in Liverpool whilst I was in my third year at Sutton High going through my A levels. The situation at Mrs Jones' was not getting any smoother, she was hostile towards me and I found her even more difficult with my sister gone, and nobody to keep her in check. Mrs Morley, the social worker, never came back so there was no opportunity to complain to anyone about how I was treated. Mrs Jones decided that I should be moved downstairs into a curtained off space on the left-hand side as one entered the hall from the front door. There was a bay window overlooking the front garden, a Sheraton table with four matching chairs in the middle of the room and a matching cabinet in the corner. The table had to be covered when doing my homework for fear of scratches. My bed, which was standing against the long wall, had to be kept pristine and tidy. It was as if I had been put in servant quarters but it was convenient when I was out for a date and came home after the curfew of 10pm. I had managed to pass quite a few of my O Levels, ten in all. I had a good memory and learning chunks of *Macbeth*, *Great Expectations*, and many poems for my English literature exam was no problem. The same was true with my general sciences and other subjects but the A levels proved to be quite a challenge. I scraped through but did not do as well as I would have hoped or expected.

My time at Sutton High School had been enjoyable but it was soon over. Three years had gone very quickly and now yet another chapter of my life was closed. I could not compete with the girls at school who had come from settled, privileged homes and were being prepared for Oxbridge. I could not be number one academically next to them, especially as I was doing everything in a different language. I had to accept it but that doesn't mean I was happy about it! I was told right from the beginning to just do my best but not to hope for too much, certainly not university. Little was expected of me. Chrysoula did see the importance of university education more than I did; I tried to escape from the predicament I found myself in by thinking I was an artist. I did a correspondence course in Art through the Athenian School of Art but I wasn't naturally artistic. My interview at Bath School of Art was a disaster. On my interview day, it was a dull afternoon and there were many young long-haired men (probably art students) milling around in the grounds. It was uncommon to see long haired men in those days and I was taken aback. I was ushered into an empty hall with a chair, small table with a pencil and paper and a mirror in the middle and I was told to draw my portrait. Never in my life had I drawn my portrait or that of anyone else! After a little while, I looked at my watch as I became suspicious of the situation – there was no one there at all, and I became rather anxious. I walked out without finishing the portrait with predictable feedback that I wasn't serious enough about a career in art, which was true enough! I never wanted to draw or paint ever again.

I decided to move on - London was beckoning. All I knew was that it was going to be different. I wanted to forge my own path and I had decided upon physiotherapy. I remembered the conversation I had heard many years ago between Rosemary Seligman and my mother when she had been talking to Mama about Chrysoula and her arm and the lack of physiotherapists on our island. A spark was ignited then. I know that what drew me was the idea of being the only one in our area to have such a position. This was what I now set my heart on.

Me at Bognoregis

Queen Elizabeth visiting Windsor Jamboree

Me at Windsor Jamboree

Chapter Fourteen

I took a gap year and, at the instigation of the social worker, I went to West London College of Commerce to take my English Cambridge Proficiency Exam which I badly needed for my physiotherapy studies. I found London daunting, huge yet lovely, but I felt very small within it and often lonely. My relationship with Chris had fizzled out. I stayed with a German family in a lovely attic apartment in Ealing Broadway. I was the grandmother's responsibility and she looked after me carefully, bringing my meals up over the weekends, whilst during the week I would join the rest of the family, consisting of her daughter, son in law, and two teenage granddaughters. They were all very pleasant people and it was a much nicer environment than that at Mrs Jones's. I remember being sick in bed for a week and they showed incredible kindness. The elderly lady became quite fond of me and I of her. She was very upset when the time came for me to leave, giving me a lovely bracelet as a present which I treasured for years.

West London College of Commerce was very different from Sutton High. There were many young people like me from the continent striving to improve their English language skills. Some of them were already with friends and in their own groups, but there was nobody from Greece or Cyprus. The large German group welcomed me and became my friends, they were great fun and very good to me.

I started to become psychologically stronger during my time in London, a great deal more confident and I think it must have been partly because I had to fend for myself completely. I was also out of the rather unsupportive, unpleasant environment of Mrs Jones. After I finished college in London, I was on the move again, this time to Liverpool, to be employed as an auxiliary nurse at Newsham General Hospital in order to gain some experience of hospital life prior to starting my physiotherapy training. Being in Liverpool would also allow me to be near Chrysoula – even though we weren't terribly close, I would at least have someone.

My train arrived at Lime Street Station late in the afternoon and I still had to buy a pair of black stockings for part of my nurse's uniform before I started work the next morning. It was just before 5pm and most of the shops were closing but, luckily, I spotted a little shop on one of the side streets, and they had what I was looking for. My shopping had delayed me somewhat and it was dark by the time I arrived at Newsham General. A group of young nurses were huddled in the staffroom, directed their attention on me as I entered. They were friendly and welcoming, their accents and dialects completely different to the Sutton High School girls.

'How many O levels have you got?' One of them asked me.

I was taken aback by the question! 'Nine or ten,' I said. There was no mention of A levels so I remained silent.

'You must be brilliant!' she said.

'Not really, not at all!' I answered, hoping that they wouldn't think I was too clever for them. That was my introduction to the hospital and to the other girls that evening.

The Newsham General Hospital in the light of the next day, was very Dickensian. Prior to becoming a hospital in 1948, it was known as the Belmond Road Workhouse, an orphanage for children who had lost their parents at sea. It consisted of three massive blocks, each of them bleak and austere. S1, S2 and S3 were the 'heavy' wards, heavy in that the patients in them were completely helpless and needed a great deal of care and attention. I was allocated to the S1 Women's Ward.

The hospital building was grey, austere and very oppressive. Most of the people in the heavy wards had Parkinson's Disseminated Sclerosis and strokes. Some were blind or deaf and everyone was just muddled together in long wards, spending their days in beds with no privacy, just thin curtains which the medical staff would sometimes draw around them. There was one woman I remember who was so big that I could hardly move her even with help. She'd had a stroke and was incredibly demanding. There was another woman who had bed sores so deep that they were down to the bone. They had to be packed and dressed and smelled badly. All of these people were on the top floor. As I climbed the long stairs, I could hear the groaning and shouting. If one asked me to describe what I imagined hell to be like, that would be it. These people were just waiting to die. I was very genteel, young and inexperienced coming from what I now realise was a sheltered and privileged background and this was all a shock to me. I could not believe that people could be treated in this way, drugged up so that they had no awareness of anything; they didn't even know what they were shouting for. It was just awful.

On my first morning, which was bitterly cold, I started my shift early. It was still winter, very dark and cold outside. I could hear the cries and screams as I ascended the long, long stairs. The stench coming from the ward was unbearable. The trained staff would take hours to pack some of the bedsores. In all my future years in various hospitals as a physio, never did I encounter cases such as those. Nursing is so different nowadays, they have hoists, hydraulic beds and other modern techniques and aids but then we had nothing, we had to physically move patients – no matter their size or condition – with nothing more than our own strength.

At the top of the stairs, at the end of the long wide corridor on the right-hand side there was a small old-fashioned kitchen. A young woman about my age was busy frying masses of bacon and sausages in an enormous frying pan. She was also an auxiliary nurse who had been employed at the hospital for a long time, probably since she left school at 14. She was confident and very much in charge, giving me orders from the outset since there were no other nurses about. I am not sure if it was because of her Liverpool dialect or maybe she had a lisp of some kind – her 't's always came out as 's', if she was saying 'night' it would come out as 'nice' – but, to me, it was an entirely different language. She was not pleased with our encounter and neither was I. It was a bit of a nightmare but I soon realised that I had to get on and help with the breakfast accepting her instructions.

I was told I had to share a room with a girl called Claire – who was just starting her career in nursing – as there was no room in the Nurse's Home. We had to occupy this room in the middle of a mile-long corridor. Claire was Irish and was the youngest of six girls with the older ones already qualified and working at the same hospital. They were a lovely, friendly bunch and full of fun. The room was large with bare walls and a high ceiling, sparsely furnished and cold looking. The one and only window was so high up the wall one couldn't see out, probably because many years ago the building had been used as an orphanage. There was a bathroom off the room with a large Victorian bath and an old, large basin. The canteen was at the end of the corridor. The two cleaners who cleaned our room would bring me my breakfast down from the canteen on my mornings off. I think they felt protective and sorry for this young, foreign girl.

Despite my poor English, I bought DH Lawrence's *Lady Chatterley's Lover*, trying to make sense of the language on my time off but I found it perverse and daring for those days. I had the book out on top of my locker next to my bed when the Matron of the hospital was doing one of her inspections. She spoke to Claire and reprimanded her for reading such a book. When Claire told her that I was reading it, she didn't believe her. I must have looked so innocent in those days!

I often joined the rest of the nurses going dancing and having great fun. I even started to smoke – that was the culture in those days. At Christmas, the Police College men were invited to the hospital dance and both Claire and I ended up pairing up with two of them – it came to nothing as most of my relationships were short-lived and exciting.

Chrysoula would occasionally come to visit me and take back to her university friends all the wrapped sweets and chocolates I had been given through the week which I couldn't keep in my two small drawers. I was popular with the patients and would chat to them during my breaks so they would reward me by giving me the many sweets which I didn't eat. Chrysoula wasn't happy with my situation and thought my living quarters and working conditions were terrible. In my spare time, I would go along to the ward and speak to patients to try and make them happy. Something they rarely got from anyone else. The whole set-up was terribly sad.

After only four months at Newsham General Hospital, I was persuaded by my sister to find another job. The Matron called me into her office.

'I'm very sad you're leaving us, Mary,' she said. 'Would you consider staying and starting your student training instead?'

'I'm afraid I have my heart set on studying physiotherapy,' I told her, and we both knew that was an end to it. Claire and her sisters, along with all the friends I had made during the last four months, were sad to see me go and I was sad to leave them behind, especially the two cleaners who had taken such good care of me.

I was on the move again.

I found a tiny room to rent in one of the old hostels in the west part of the city and began desperately looking for another job. I had very little money left since I refused any assistance from home. I thought I could easily manage during my gap year but couldn't even afford to buy an airmail envelope to send to my mother. The hostel was large and bare, the dining room full of long, narrow tables where I shared my meal with some students. I went up and down Lime Street relentlessly, I could have got a factory job but this did not appeal. Eventually I spotted a sign saying 'Lucie Clayton'. I didn't really know what this place was but I thought I would investigate a little further.

I climbed the long stairs and I was greeted at the top by a woman in her forties.

'I'm looking for a job,' I told her as soon as I entered.

She looked me up and down approvingly.

'Come over here,' she told me, coldly. 'Stand on these scales.'

It was an odd request, but I was young and naïve, and felt that I should do as she asked. Once I had been weighed, she walked away and picked up a measuring tape from her desk.

'Arms up,' she demanded, measuring my bust, then moving on to my waist and hips. How strange! The woman became nicer to me once she had all of my details and told me that Lucie Clayton was one of the top model agencies in the country and she was keen to take me on. That seemed like quite a positive outcome to my peculiar meeting until she informed me that there would be a £20 fee for training purposes.

I met my sister and future brother-in-law, Norman, later that day and told them what had happened.

'That sounds like a great opportunity,' Norman said. 'I'll happily lend you the money.'

It did sound fantastic so I thanked him and said I would look for a job for one more day, just in case there was something better. Just behind the Adelphi Hotel, I stumbled across a large building which I later learned was a big complex of Reeces, housing cafes, restaurants, bakers and retail offices for the Wirral Dairy. I climbed up a long stair and on my right there was an enormous room full of people working at their desks. This was the Accounts Department of Reeces.

'Can I help you?' a woman asked.

'May I see the manager please?' I replied.

I was shown into the Manager's Office and he asked me to take a seat in one of the corners opposite him.

'Tell me about yourself,' he said. 'what do you think you could do here.'

I told him a bit about my school and my auxiliary nursing experience and that I had been looking for a job the last two or three days without any success. I said that I did have the opportunity with the Lucie Clayton Agency but not the money for training.

'No, my dear,' he said. 'Nice girls like you don't go into that sort of thing. I'll give you a job.'

I was delighted even if I had perhaps passed up my chance to become the next Jean Shrimpton! I found myself in the Accounts Department (accounts and maths were not quite my forte), sitting at a desk next to a small Irish lady in her forties called Peggy. Peggy was extremely helpful and pleasant. She proceeded to teach me the ropes, everything to do with numbers and accounts. I was taken to an enormous canteen for my break, full of young men from the bakery and other departments. I must have looked very different as everybody seemed to stare at me and I felt a little uneasy.

'It's because of your sunny smile, Maria,' Peggy told me. 'You are a ray of sunshine.' I thanked her for the compliment but was still very self-conscious. This is the time I'd found the confidence to start calling myself Maria, never Maro or Mary, but there were still many steps on the path before I would truly feel I could be myself.

Things started looking up. I was meeting people of my own age. Chrysoula invited me to meet the girls she was sharing halls with and also to some social events at the University. It was at one of these socials that I met Christos and Marios from Cyprus. Christos asked me out and we planned to meet up with three or four of his friends at the famous Blue Angel where The Beatles, The Rolling Stones, Bob Dylan, and many other bands played in the 1960s.

We were all having a great time when a friend of Christos - known as Graham the Scotsman - started giving me too much attention. He was asking me for my phone number and address and would not take 'no' for an answer.

Some normality was established once the meal finished and we all went to another club for a hot chocolate. When the time came to leave, the other boys wouldn't let him join us in the car. He was left standing on the pavement without my address or phone number which he had been after all night!

A few days after that episode, I happened to be walking past The Adelphi Hotel carrying a full basket of books and walking towards the library when Graham approached, walking towards me. His face was beaming and extremely happy to see me so unexpectedly. I said, 'I am off to the library – are you going that way as well?'

'Yes, yes I am!' he beamed.

I don't know how this could have been as he had been walking towards me! He got a hold of my heavy basket of books and we walked on, chatting and happy to be together. He seemed much less pushy now that we were alone together. He sat on the bench at the back of the room in the library, listening to the exchange of conversation between me and the librarian, quite amused by what was going on. I think she was trying to explain that the books were overdue and that I had to pay some money. I didn't understand and, at the end, she let me off.

'Would you go out with me this evening?' Graham asked. He wasn't missing any opportunity this time. I agreed and we went out to dinner that night where the time passed too quickly. Christos was furious. He phoned me the next day saying I was crazy to go out with Graham.

'He's not good enough for you!' he claimed.

I didn't take much notice as I had heard that line too many times in my life and continued to see Graham. He said that he was working at the bank meantime but was planning to go back to university. He had been at Leicester University, two or three years prior but not enjoyed what he was doing, so he dropped out. He was planning to go back to Scotland. His mother was originally from Edinburgh and his father from Perth. Although he lived in Liverpool, he was very attached to his Scottish roots - he used to visit his aunt in Edinburgh who instilled in him very strong feelings for Scotland from when he was still very young. Later, when at Strathclyde University, he started the first Nationalists club – I thought he was crazy! I don't think I ever really looked into my feelings about this aspect of Graham's personality – I had seen the damage and the horror, of nationalism back home, and yet here was a man who thought highly of such things. I think I separated the two but it is a very interesting question – why was I with a man who had such views when my young life was ruined? I think I could only believe that they were different things and just thought he was crazy then. *Let the boy play*, I thought – and I would think that about so many things in our life with what he wanted.

Picture taken not long after getting engaged to Graham

Chapter Fifteen

I met Graham in the spring of that year but I'm afraid it was not quite love at first sight. I wasn't quite sure of my feelings and not very serious – perhaps I was rather spoiled. I think I had too much attention from the opposite sex throughout the years.

By June, Cyprus was beckoning. I decided to leave Reeces for my great journey home as I felt my time there was at a natural end. I had been very happy at Reeces and my colleagues were sad to see me go. I was showered with many presents and farewells. I particularly missed Peggy as she had been my rock. Graham was very upset to say goodbye, but I promised to write to him and see him on my return in August.

In the meantime, I managed to secure two physiotherapy places, one in Glasgow and the other in Portsmouth. One in Glasgow at the Scottish School of Physiotherapy, which was closely connected to Glasgow University at the time and the other at Portsmouth Naval School of Physiotherapy. I was particularly pleased to be accepted here as this was quite an achievement considering they mostly only took on men as students and only one or two women. However, I chose Glasgow as Graham was planning to apply for a place there and felt the Glasgow physiotherapy school's connections to the university was quite appealing. All the professional subjects and exams in anatomy, physiology, pathology and electrotherapy were held at the university, but before that, I had my summer back home.

Chrysoula and I went through Europe by train, spending some time in Venice where we boarded an Italian boat to cross the Mediterranean. I was eighteen years old then, the world was my oyster. I was reaching for the stars for sure. I had a wonderful time on my journey back to Cyprus. I met up with an Italian officer with whom I thought I fell in love, had dinner at the Captain's table, and danced all night, so different from my first journey to England. Graham was becoming but a distant memory and so was my father's murder.

I was delighted to be with my mother and siblings again, it was very moving. I was amused to see how they had all shot up in height, including my youngest brother, Sotiris. He had no speech but his little face was beaming and he was pleased to see us back. The poor boy, he was so heavily dependent on Mama. My youngest sister, Thea, was a pretty little girl with fair, curly hair who spent a lot of time playing with the many wild cats and kittens in the garden. Thea got attached to Chrysoula whilst Despo, about ten years of age was definitely my friend. Such a sweet girl, extremely bright with a sparkle in her eyes, Despo was probably the most intelligent of us all – she would go on to study architecture in London, in the school of architecture in the Architecture Association (AA). She gained her PhD and ultimately became a Professor at Cyprus University of Technology. My brother Andreas was 14 when we went back, also a good-looking boy, and very much in charge of the household. There were no teenage hang-ups about him, he was sociable, talkative and always helpful. He also went on to do architecture and developed a thriving business in Cyprus.

All of my siblings did well despite the odds. None of us went through the usual torments and aggression of the teenage years, we just had no time for that and I think that was because of what we had been through. That summer, we all knew somehow what all of us would become and it was a wonderful time.

Mother was pleased to see us all together, as was my cousin Andreas, eight years my senior who would often be my chaperone. One of the most memorable occasions together was at Zephyros, the night club in the beautiful setting which I mentioned earlier in my story. It overlooked the Mediterranean Sea with amazing, commanding views from every aspect. There were many steps going down to a secluded bay where we would go for a swim, and there were beautiful grounds and gardens.

On that particular Saturday night which I remember well, there was a big event taking place. Miss Lemoni, the Queen of the Lemons, was going to be chosen. The whole Kyrenian district was famous for its production and export of lemons, and every year, the most beautiful girl was chosen as Miss Lemoni.

Andreas, my cousin, was very fashionable and handsome, he was dressed in an off-white Italian evening suit whereas I was wearing a most becoming silk, sea-blue, fitted raffled dress, a designer dress with thin straps over the shoulders. I had spent my last penny buying it just before I left England, I just loved that dress. It was an incredible evening. I met lots of people I knew and danced all night. I was particularly pleased to dance with Tefcros, a young man who I was crazy about – although I thought Graham was perfectly nice, I wasn't in love with him as yet and I was much more attracted to Tefcros. He was one of my cousin's group but younger than the rest of his friends. His father had been one of my teachers in my fifth year of primary school and Tefcros had wanted to marry me at one point. He was extremely intelligent and, at the time, had just finished studying for his Civil Engineering degree as he had been put ahead by a year.

The night was magical. I danced the last dance with my cousin before the voting started for choosing Miss Lemoni. There were masses of people there and they chose me by a large majority. I never felt so happy in all my life. Me, chosen by the people! I just couldn't believe it.

I received a solid gold brooch with 'Miss Lemoni' engraved at the top and little golden lemons, with leaves dangling down, dinner for two at a famous restaurant and a hairdo at an exclusive hair salon. Mama was so happy! People were giving me a lot of attention, staring and talking about me and wanting to be near me. Some, of course, were extremely jealous but I ignored them. I was floating on air.

The rest of my holiday was disappearing fast. Uncle Panayiotis, who became our guardian on our father's death, wanted to talk to me. 'Maro,' he said, 'many young men will want to marry you, please do not end up marrying just anyone from over there.' Mama repeated that request – marrying a foreigner would be a disaster. I didn't give it much thought at the time as I had no intention of marrying yet anyway. We said our last goodbyes and this time we flew back to Britain, tears were rolling down my face as the outline of Cyprus disappeared into the distance. That summer had been the best of my life. I was going back to Britain with some trepidation. Glasgow was looming on the horizon. I didn't know what to expect – the only thing I knew was that there would be a lot of hard work.

My physiotherapy colleagues appeared to be a pleasant bunch, most of them found the medical terminology difficult to understand as if they were learning a foreign language. A great deal of the vocabulary used in medicine derived from ancient Greek and Latin and having studied Advanced Level

Greek, it was a walk in the park to me. My good memory and knowledge of the medical terms soon helped to bring me to the top of my year. I got a record-breaking distinction in all of my professional exams at Glasgow University. My English language had improved a great deal by then despite some of the hiccups I had understanding the Glaswegian dialect! Everything I had known with regards to my education prior to my father's murder had been completely wiped out when I arrived in England and left me at a huge disadvantage but now I was flying high. There are a great number of children in the world who find themselves in similar situations and the vicious cycle of trauma and circumstances become perpetuated. I was fortunate to escape.

When I first started my studies, I stayed at St Mary's Hostel in Wilton Street, a long street running between Kelvinside – an exclusive part of Glasgow – and Maryhill, a disadvantaged area. The hostel was nearer to Maryhill Road, where there was a cluster of shops such as a bakery, butcher, and a grocery, all of which I used to frequent. At the other end of the street was the BBC building. The hostel was a large Georgian building occupying a good stretch of Wilton Street Crescent, a dozen steps leading up from the road to the entrance where a large statue of St Mary stood there to greet you. Another door opened up from a hall to various corridors going in all directions. The hostel was run by the Sisters of Charity who did everything – the cleaning, the cooking, and generally looking after all of us. At the far end of the main corridor, on the right-hand side, a few steps led to the chapel. Every evening, the nuns, one after the other, in their traditional Catholic habits, all black down to their ankles and their headwear, the Cornette, resembling large white horns on either side of the head, would silently and solemnly walk towards the chapel for their prayers. The first time I saw them I stopped in my tracks, bowed my head and waited until they were out of sight.

Long narrow stairs led down to massive dark rooms and corridors in the basement used for domestic purposes. One of them was used as the laundry room, sparsely furnished with an old-fashioned mangle and an ancient washing machine, very frightening in the long, dark winter evenings. When on my own, I could feel the presence of spirits scampering about. Further along the corridor, tucked out of sight, was the kitchen where the nuns prepared our meals. A strong smell of overcooked vegetables, mostly cabbage and cauliflower, would drift up to the entrance and as soon as I would open the front door, a smell similar to that of formaldehyde, a chemical used to preserve bodies in the dissection room at Glasgow University for our Practical Anatomy training, would pervade the air. Our lecturer, Dr Warbrick, remained composed and amused as one by one my female colleagues dropped, fainting, on the floor, overwhelmed by the 'formaldehyde' and the general atmosphere of the dissection room with bodies on the trolleys, scattered about for dissection. My room at the hostel, was lovely overlooking the Crescent, green with trees and with railings all around. It was a good-size room, well furnished, with an en-suite bathroom. I was on the same floor as a Miss MacDonald, a rather strange woman in her fifties whom I thought quite elderly at the time. She was very private and never ventured out of her room. The nuns did everything for her. I suspect she was suffering from some form of mental illness. At first, I was a little frightened and worried being on the same landing and made sure my door was always locked. In those days, like many of my contemporaries, I was suspicious and frightened of any form of mental illness which I now regret very much – and, of course, rather ironically having gained an Honours in Psychology a few years later.

One afternoon, on my way to my room, I saw her door half-opened with Miss MacDonald sitting in an armchair just opposite the top of the stairs. I smiled at her and said 'Hello.' I proceeded to introduce myself and to my great surprise, she responded by asking me which country I came from and we struck up a little conversation. I wonder now if perhaps she suffered from severe depression. After our initial introduction, I always tried to greet her and speak to her whenever I got the chance or whenever her door was slightly open, which was not often but she remained remote, with the nuns bringing her meals up and looking after her. Maybe she was a nun herself or had been prior to her illness.

A short time after my arrival in Glasgow and whilst staying at the hostel, my Mother wanted to pay me a visit along with my brother, Sotiris, who must have been about 10 years old by then. I was happy about the prospect of seeing them both and said I would organise their accommodation. I duly knocked on Mother Superior's office door. A portly, homely serious woman was sitting in front of a large desk absorbed in her work, she pointed to a chair opposite and asked me to explain the purpose of my visit. I told her about my Mother and brother's visit and my brother's speech and learning difficulties.

'No, males cannot stay at the hostel,' she said, flatly. My eyes filled with tears as I got up and readied to leave the room. She stopped me with a hand movement. 'I will make an exception for you Maria,' she said. 'I'll get them a nice room.' I was very pleased with the outcome and Mama loved the place. She was a devout Greek Orthodox and was delighted to see the statue of Mother Mary at the entrance, where she stopped and crossed herself several times.

Mama was absolutely amazed to see great expanses of land planted here and there with unproductive trees rather than useful fruit bearing ones as she was used to in Cyprus.

Everyone was helpful and understanding with my brother and their stay with me was memorable for all three of us. Their room, although at the other end of the hostel quite some distance from mine, was perfect in every way. I would visit them as soon as I got back each day from university. After a long walk along Great Western Road, up the steep Belmont Street and along Wilton Street. I was exhausted by the time I climbed the stairs to their room. They joined in with the life at the hostel and I even took them for a trip to Loch Lomond. My mother loved Scotland and enthused about it for years to come.

I was settling well in Glasgow and I found the Scots friendly and appealing, somewhat different from their cousins further south I thought. Graham visited me on his big Honda motorbike all the way from Liverpool several times and stayed at a bed and breakfast in Kelvinside. He was head over heels in love with me. I started looking forward to his visits and missed him terribly when gone. For the first time in my life, I was settled. I was doing well with my studies, I had plenty of friends, despite the fact Graham was becoming rather possessive and over-protective, desperate to put a ring on my finger.

My sister Chrysoula finished her studies at Liverpool University that summer and was getting married to her boyfriend Norman who she had been with since Fresher's Day at University. They had a big, elaborate wedding in the Greek Orthodox church in Manchester; Mother, brother Sotiris and Auntie Irene all came to the wedding. I was one of the three bridesmaids and Graham was one of the three best men. We all stayed in a big house in Didsbury, a suburban area on the north bank of the river Mersey, about four and a half miles south of Manchester city centre, where we enjoyed some lovely walks in the countryside and by the riverbank. Graham was starting to be seen as my boyfriend by many of them at that point.

Chrysoula and Norman left for Indiana to pursue further studies as Norman had a scholarship to undertake a PhD and Chrysoula was to study for her Masters. A good few years later, Chrysoula also got her PhD from London. Mother met Graham for the first time at the wedding and I had a suspicion that she was not very enthusiastic about him. He had a 'roving eye' she said, but, as always, she was diplomatic and kept silent. She did not try to influence me in any way. Perhaps she knew it was far too late to interfere.

Our engagement was announced soon after my sister and Norman left for America and Auntie Irene went back to Cyprus. I felt committed in our relationship and did say 'yes' when Graham asked me to marry him. When I met his family for the first time, it was extremely uncomfortable. Heather, his sister, together with a friend, were listening to music when Graham first took me to meet his family. She turned to Graham and said, 'Take her out – she wouldn't understand my music!'

He was clearly the black sheep and they had little affection for him. Graham never got on well with his mother or sister, Heather. He was an outsider, completely frozen out and his mother always put him down for some reason. She was particularly resentful when he did better than his sister. She suggested repeatedly that he should do a primary school teaching course like his sister rather than pursue university. His mother and sister had a kind of symbiotic relationship and although they would fight like cat and dog, they would protect the interests of each other up to the end. Although successful in her career, Heather never left the family home or made an independent life for herself. Graham was left nothing in her will, but his mother asked Graham, me and our children to look after Heather when she died.

Graham's father was a sweet man but unfortunately, he had Parkinson's disease and passed away in his 70s. Having fought in both world wars, the stress on his nervous system was too much to bear. He was a quiet man, his wife and daughter did all the talking, he just listened and complied. They were not particularly hospitable to my people either. Mother overheard them saying, 'What strange people they are!' Poor Graham - it must have been difficult to keep on fighting your corner when your own mother is your greatest adversary. He had a bad childhood, leaving him with issues in his adult life and he was rather insecure. He had to fight for everything – there was no way he would let me go. I felt from the moment Graham met me, he felt as if he had found something, someone, just for him and he would hold onto me with all his might.

My cousin Andreas with his wife and sisters

Chapter Sixteen

Our wedding was to take place the following summer. There was to be a Registry Office wedding on the 29th of June followed by a Greek Orthodox Church wedding on the 6th of July. My future mother-in-law wanted to have the wedding day for people she knew and was very unwelcoming to me and my friends, Betsy and Lily Lee, lovely girls from Malaya who were also studying physio in Glasgow and who were my bridesmaids. She knew that Heather would never marry, probably because she didn't want her to and I feel that she didn't want my special day to be too nice as her daughter would never experience the same.

My family couldn't come to my wedding as the distance was too great in those days. Besides, we were to see them all during our honeymoon for another big celebration. My Mother sent me a very personal letter, which I still have and treasure, saying how much she regretted not being there and, in a poem, which she composed, she wished us all the best for our great day.

My mother-in-law was rather controlling and unpleasant to me, but quite able. At first, she would have wondered why on earth her son was involved with me. In those days, there was more suspicion of people from different cultures so I found this understandable. Luckily, they all lived in Liverpool, some distance away from Glasgow. I was half-hearted about the white wedding and I would have rather just had the Registry Office ceremony but it was very important to my mother. Even though she would not be able to attend, she knew that only a Greek Orthodox ceremony would be valid in her eyes and those of friends and family back in Cyprus. When one of my bridesmaids to be had to pull out very close to the day, I was quite upset. I asked my sister-in-law if she would step in, but she wouldn't but Betsy and Lily Lee were true friends and saved the day by stepping in at the last minute.

There was nobody to give me away apart from an acquaintance of Graham's sister who was a pleasant man, very comical, in the same teaching college year as Heather some years before. Alec wasn't really a close family friend and it was kind of him to take this role, but for me it was just another odd addition to what should have been the happiest day of my life. In the back of the wedding car, all of a sudden, I started to cry. He tried to make me feel better but my heart was heavy. I was very young, I was in another country, and I was about to face a very cold wedding – I looked out of the window, not wanting him to see my eyes filling with tears, but the tears ran down my face just the same.

As we continued the journey to the church I reflected on the ideas which had been around me when I was a child and a young woman. There was a real change in expectations and the ambition of my mother's generation, to be the perfect wife and mother, was not mine. I and my sister had always expected to marry but also to strive for something, to be someone, and to be self-sufficient. When we were young girls, women in Cyprus were generally not educated and even in the UK, further education for women was the exception rather than the rule. Most wives stayed at home and relied on marriage to a man of substance rather than expecting to be the beneficiaries of their own effort and achievements. We had to comply with the culture: that was the background to my life. As I became of age in Cyprus, it was strange to see my mother being approached to ask whether I would be interested in marriage. Permission was still asked of the parent rather than the young woman. I learned to live like an English girl in my teenage years. If I had stayed in Karavas, there would have been a dowry, there would have been an accepted approach of marriage at some point. The old ways seemed so alien to me once I was in the UK. I tried to reason with myself - I was marrying a man I had chosen, no one had forced me or even suggested to me that I should do so, and I was completely responsible for my choices even if sometimes I felt obligated to go through with them.

We arrived at church. The ceremony was in Greek, and the guests of course were all English, with nobody of my own except for my two bridesmaids.

Not long after the ceremony began, the priest gave Graham a sip of the wine and a bite of the bread. It was so quick, and he didn't really know what to do as we didn't have a trial run or rehearsal beforehand. Graham must have taken too big a bite instead of just a small piece, and he choked. Poor Graham didn't realise that the bread and sips of wine, not gulps, offered by the priest was to be repeated three times, not just once. I was so full of nerves, just at breaking point, and I started to laugh. Imagine a bride laughing at her groom choking! The giggles were coming out of me and everyone was staring. The more I tried to control my giggles and laughter, the worse it was. The priest was serious, he just carried on, but I was ready to burst with laughter.

The rest of the wedding was alright – that is about all the enthusiasm I could muster for it. We stayed at a local hotel afterwards and, absolutely exhausted by the day's events, I collapsed onto the bed and into a deep sleep.

The next day, we travelled to London and then to Dover for the boat over to Calais and the train through Europe, stopping here and there. We visited Cologne, Athens, and Alexandria, just missing a devastating earthquake at Skopje going through Yugoslavia. We boarded the boat for Cyprus at Piraeus, a completely different journey to my previous ones in every way. Everyone was delighted to see us when we finally arrived. We had a big celebration on the veranda and got masses of presents in recognition of our wedding. My cousins invited us to their houses for meals piled high with Greek food and delicacies which they spent hours preparing and which they knew were my favourites. Much to their disappointment, and mine, all of a sudden, I couldn't face any food. I was feeling nauseated, I was not my usual self. I was in fact pregnant with Moina, my first child, a honeymoon baby after the Registry Office wedding.

It was still so beautiful in Cyprus but there were even more changes coming, although I did not have the awareness of this in the same way as those who lived there. We went to visit my godmother who was a very wise lady. She had big blue eyes which was very unusual in Cyprus as most people had brown and she was very old-fashioned, always wrapped up with scarves concealing her tiny body. She was living with her daughter Irene who had been prevented from being my godmother because she had been menstruating during the time of the washing of the baptism linen.

I said to her, 'We have spotted a lovely site overlooking the sea, on the west side of Cyprus. It is so beautiful with views over the rocks – I think we would like to buy it.'

I thought she would be pleased that we had plans to come back to Cyprus and settle at some point, but her face clouded over.

'No, Maro, no – don't do that.'

'Why?' I asked her in surprise.

'I am afraid that the Turks will invade and take it all. We will be left with nothing, do not plan your future here because there may be no future to plan.'

She knew. A premonition? Perhaps – or maybe she had heard things. We took her advice on board and did not make plans to settle there after all.

The holiday in Cyprus rolled by very quickly. I took Graham to various sights of interest, which he loved. I was now a married woman with a child on the way and my life would be completely different. I was to start my second year of studies in the middle of August and had to be back soon. I managed to sell some of my property from my father's inheritance to buy a good second floor apartment in Wilton Drive in Glasgow, almost directly opposite the window of my room at the hostel and I tried to carry on as before. Graham was to start his studies in Economics at Strathclyde in September, as a mature student. I often felt nauseated and unwell but I put on a brave face. I was slim and most people weren't aware of my pregnancy. Unbelievably, I was over seven months when a charity float manned by medical students kidnapped me from college premises in my uniform. They just didn't believe me when I said I was pregnant and would they please put me down? One of my friends had to make a lot of fuss before they finally did. It took me a long time before I calmed down as I was really shaken.

We were completely unprepared when the baby arrived three weeks earlier than anticipated. A lovely little girl was born to us at the Rottenrow Maternity Hospital. We called her Moina. She had a mass of long black hair and was such a dear little thing. She was jaundiced but certainly had a good pair of lungs! My in-laws arrived at our house on our first day back. Both of them were full of cold, and my poor father-in-law was finding it difficult to get about due to his Parkinson's which was getting worse. There was nothing to eat in the house, my husband was running here and there, achieving nothing. I have always been a coper, but the situation was going from bad to worse. The baby suffered from colic and didn't like sleeping at all. I tried to follow the health visitor's advice and gave her lots of gripe water, but it didn't help especially given that I was, as a first-time mother, left feeling that I was being watched and judged all of the time by my in-laws.

Things improved a little when all of the visitors went away and I tried to get into some sort of routine. However, the baby continued to be unsettled overnight and we continued fussing over her. After a week I returned to my studies and, during the day, Moina was taken to the local nursery on Maryhill Road.

The Number 41 bus from Kelvinside was shaky and the journey rather uneasy. Walking from the bus stop to the college was a nightmare – all I could do was pray I wouldn't pass out.

Everyone was amazed to see me back: my figure was almost back to normal, and many of my colleagues couldn't understand what was happening as they hadn't even known I was pregnant. Life was difficult though. There wasn't any help in those days if there was no family nearby and I had to quickly learn some parenting skills. It was very useful having the local nursery but I did have to juggle a great many demands.

Moina grew fast and was an intelligent little girl. A psychologist apparently did some tests with the children in day-care and I was told by the nursery manager that we had an unusually bright child. I was soon introduced to nursery rhymes, something I had never heard of until then. I bought her baby books and everything was going well until one day on collecting her I was told we couldn't take her back there again because the children of students weren't allowed to be registered any more. We were devastated and had to take turns looking after Moina until we managed to find a babysitter. Mrs McDonald lived quite near us and was a qualified nurse who needed some extra income. She was a big lady, serious and strict with Moina and her own little boy, Callum. I'm sorry to say that she was not a very pleasant woman, but we were desperate.

The three friends I made at the college were particularly helpful. Joe, Helena and Liz would often come up to babysit at the weekends to let me go out with Graham. My friends enjoyed playing with the baby and loved the delicious cakes I would buy for them from this amazing bakery on Maryhill Road. However, they soon got tied down with boyfriends and relationships of their own, and babysitting was cut to a minimum if any at all.

My husband had finished his studies by now and was doing his teaching diploma at Glasgow University and Jordanhill. Sadly, he started spending his Friday evenings with the boys singing and drinking at the union bar which was clearly more enjoyable than being stuck at home with me and a baby. I was feeling quite low at times, revisiting memories and thoughts, thinking of what I'd hoped my life would be and wondering if I would ever reach the heights of which I knew I was capable.

I finished my studies with distinctions in most of my professional subjects and almost immediately got a part-time job at the Glasgow Bath Street Clinic and Knightswood Hospital to tide us over until Graham finished his teaching qualification. He then got his first appointment as a lecturer at the College of Further Education in Inverness. We were living in St Valery Avenue at the time, in a council house until we bought one of our own. Moina was three by then, a sweet girl but quite hyperactive. With any opportunity, she would run away. One day she disappeared with one of her little friends, Amanda, for quite a while. I immediately panicked as the canal was quite near us and I thought they were perhaps near to there. I called the police and just when a large crowd had gathered, two little ones, hand in hand, appeared strolling back after visiting the town cemetery!

My youngest sister Thea came to stay with us – she attended the Academy School for a year and then went to London where Mama, Despo and Sotiris now lived with Chrysoula, her husband and their little boy Adrian in the large, Tudor style house in Chigwell which Mama had helped them buy. It was an extensive residence with an acre of garden and a massive orchard. Sotiris was sent to a special school somewhere in London, I don't know exactly where it was located. Apparently, he desperately tried to make friends with the other children who also had learning difficulties but the language was too much of a handicap – on many occasions he even tried to make friends by giving his lunch away but nothing helped.

Sotiris was pushing a wheelbarrow around the garden one day when he got knocked on the knee. The joint became increasingly painful, swollen and inflamed. Unfortunately, this was the beginning of an osteoma, bone cancer of the knee and in a few months he was dead. He was only 12 years old at the time. Looking back, he was a sweet, helpful, kind young boy and it must have been so difficult for him to be in this new culture without any speech or knowledge of the language. Mama was devastated – Sotiris was her third son to die and her youngest child.

When we lived at Wilton Drive in Glasgow, it was a very friendly atmosphere – the people were very kind. As soon as the manager of the local grocery shop would see me and Moina walking through the always open door, she would survey the long rows of apples beautifully arranged according to variety and colour on the right-hand side wall, pick up the rosiest of them, shine it on her dirty apron and hand it over to Moina. My little girl used to love living there, the people were so friendly and kind to us, but when we next moved – to Inverness – sadly, there was not the same open-hearted, friendly environment. Inverness itself was lovely but I did not feel quite as welcomed there. In Glasgow, the environment had been much more multi-cultural and. Of course, Glaswegians are renowned for their friendliness.

Almost as soon as I got a job at Raigmore Hospital, I discovered that I was pregnant again with my second daughter, Fiona. She was still a baby when I was headhunted by the Red Cross to work with young people with physical disabilities. This was a part time position, but I was also approached by a private concern to treat disabled children under five years of age. Both employers had support in place to look after Fiona whilst I was busy working but a time was coming where that would be the least of my worries.

Chapter Seventeen

Fiona was nine months old when I had another setback in my life. I had a terrible car accident on my way to work. It was the first of April, the snow started falling and there was a thin covering of white on the roads. I was trying to negotiate a bad bend in the heart of Inverness, Culduthel Road, when a learner scooter driver suddenly appeared in front of me swaying here and there. He slowed down suddenly and when I tried to overtake him, my little Mini skidded from one side of the road to the other. At first, I thought I would hit the high stone wall on my left, but then my car swung to the right, collided with a double decker bus. I can't remember much after that apart from vaguely recalling the screeching and hooting of the ambulance and hearing myself calling for my mother. I lost consciousness and woke up in hospital surrounded by doctors and nurses, still wearing my cerise spring coat and having no feeling in my left leg.

'Have I got all my limbs?' I asked.

'Everything is there,' a disembodied voice replied before I passed out again. I was in the Intensive Care Unit of Raigmore Hospital. I had fractured a couple of my ribs, pelvis, and a vertebra. My left hip joint was completely dislocated, severing the ligamentum Teres artery connecting the head of the femur to the acetabulum, which meant that there would be no supply of blood to the joint and it would get arthritic sooner rather than later. The pain was unbearable, and I was put in traction for a long time.

On his ward round the next day, Mr Frew the orthopaedic surgeon, said, 'It's just as well you're a physio!' I did not appreciate his comment at the time, but he was absolutely right. I was particularly upset about the cut between my eyebrows. It looked horrendous. However, every cloud has a silver lining. My husband was starting his Easter vacation that morning, so Fiona was not with me as usual. Normally she would have come to work with me to be looked after by the people there. I still had my Fiona alive, my lovely baby girl of only nine months had been spared.

My accident hit the headlines the next morning there was a picture of my little Mini, a wreck of crumpled up metal in front of the double decker bus which had very little damage. The caption read, *How could anybody come out of this alive?* Even knowing I had been the one who had come out alive, the only answer I had was that it must have been my mother's prayers which saved me.

Mama came up from London to look after both children, Moina and Fiona but had to leave as soon as I was out of hospital, something to do with Andreas, my brother, getting ready for his Military Service. I got very depressed and couldn't cope – being on crutches and looking after the baby was very hard. Prior to my accident I had sold yet another chunk of my inheritance to buy a house in a pleasant area of Inverness. Number 30 Green Drive was a 1930s property which needed to be completely gutted and an extension built. At the time of the accident everything was in chaos and more like a builder's yard than a home. My husband spent his time trying to do the house up while working full time as a lecturer which meant that domestic responsibilities for him were out of the question.

Fiona was an easy-going child, well-behaved, calm, sleeping well overnight. I persevered with everything despite having little or no domestic support. I had always been a fighter and saw no reason to stop. I practised my walking for hours on end in the long back garden and did my self-physio every day, binning the anti-depressants not wishing to become dependent on them but also knowing that I could not allow myself the luxury of simply resting and waiting for everything to become better – no, I would have to work hard for everything I wanted, my family, my health, my job. I had a good recovery considering the experts gloomy prediction that I would never walk again but I did have to battle for it very hard indeed. I returned to work, throwing the crutches away. The people at the Red Cross and the volunteers of the under-five group were excellent at helping me and I appreciated that very much.

Fiona was barely two years old when we were on the move again when Graham got a promotion and we headed south to Perth. We stayed temporarily in a council house while our new house was being built at Kinnoull, a very pleasant residential area in the city. I loved the new house and made many friends quite quickly, I found Perth friendly and welcoming. Although I was still limping and often in pain, I got a part time job with the NHS at Hillside Hospital, just down the road from our house. I worked with chronically sick people, a job which suited me well. I soon became pregnant with my third child, Sophie, but got back to work a month after she was born, having to organise babysitters and trying to get on with my life.

Graham was very unhappy at work. There were arguments and discontent throughout the college. The little department Graham was in charge of when we first moved to Perth expanded considerably and the Principal decided to restructure, splitting it up and putting in charge someone who would look after everything overall. There was a great deal of competition and squabbling and Graham did not get the position.

Sophie was two to three months old when Graham managed to get a year's sabbatical to study for his Masters of Education at Dundee University. My husband was never very good at studying despite the fact that he was very intelligent. I had to push him all the way so that he could achieve his best. It was indeed a very difficult year and Graham was definitely going through a mid-life crisis. The family responsibilities were becoming too much for him and he wanted time out just to study. He left for the West of Scotland carrying his books with him, to get some time alone away from the children and the demands of home – I stayed behind to work, and raise the girls and the baby, and to continue making life as good as possible for our family. Graham's plans did not last for long as the good weather was too tempting in the beautiful West. He spent his time on boat trips, making friends with the boatman, going over to the island of Kerrera and having what was really a rather good holiday free of responsibility. Studying was the last thing on his mind, and he came back after two or three weeks, as disgruntled as ever.

On his return, the winter was creeping in and Graham was getting more and more anxious about his studies, he said that he could not concentrate at home, so he moved to Dundee where he lived in the Halls of Residence. I let him carry on with whatever he was supposedly doing. This was not something I wished to fight over as I had so many plates to spin anyway. Just before I had fallen pregnant with Sophie, I had started studying with the Open University for my psychology degree. It took me some time to get back to studying after the baby was born, and it was a lot to juggle given that Graham was having another crisis and had all but checked out of our family life, but soon my Cs turned into Bs and my Bs into As for my assignments. When Sophie was a little baby, I would get up early in the morning, 5am, to bathe her, feed her, settle her down and then study until the rest of the house started to stir. This was my routine and I had to keep it going no matter what.

Moina, my eldest, was ten years old by this time and a great help to me. She was a very able and intelligent child, helping me with the baby a great deal. I was too preoccupied with the children, house and husband to let anything else worry me so I didn't allow myself that luxury – I was too busy. Graham was trying to emulate the young students, reliving his youth. He would come home over some weekends, wearing a pair of light purple flared trousers and I was slightly irritated when he said that I should get some sexy underwear! As if I had time for that! My husband was intelligent, there is no doubt of that, but he suffered terribly from anxiety finding it difficult to actually get down to any studying.

Soon the end of the university year came around, with its inevitable exams. Graham came home at that time and travelled every morning to Dundee for his exams, equipped with a tape recorder to listen to his notes in the car, during his journey. Miraculously, he managed to pass the exams despite all the odds. He got his Masters, which was just as well, for if he had failed, he would never have been able to face his colleagues again. He went back to the College in Autumn but unfortunately the situation had become even more trying. His higher qualification did not make anything better, in fact it made things worse. The Perth College of Further Education was not an especially academic institution at the time and to have a degree was a rarity. Most of the other departmental heads had technical qualifications in building, plumbing, catering and others. I imagine having a Master's in Education was more of a hindrance than a ticket to promotion and seen as somewhat threatening.

Sophie was nine months old when I was asked to apply for a full-time position as a Senior II at Perth Royal Infirmary (PRI). I put her in the nursery - she was a lovely little child but quite demanding. It was difficult but I pushed on, my new job was challenging, and I had to learn a great deal more than I had anticipated. I attended a few courses and wrote a thesis in order to get my postgraduate qualification in Obstetrics and Gynaecology. After a little while, I was put in charge of all the general wards and became Deputy to the Superintendent, with somebody else taking over my obstetrics and gynaecology work. This new role lasted for a few years when I went back to my original work being a specialist physio in Obstetrics and Gynaecology. This paid just as well with less responsibility for staff and their management. I had found it difficult being in charge – you are not one of a group anymore and it can feel lonely. One of the female physios gave me a particularly rough time. When one day I asked her to tell me exactly what the problem was, she simply said, 'I don't like having a woman boss.' I said that was indeed her problem.

On the whole, I enjoyed my work at PRI. I got to know many people throughout the hospital and probably most of Perth as patients or people connected to them, whether in gynaecology, having babies, or outpatients. There was even a big article in the 'Dundee Courier' about my achievements, listing all of my responsibilities and praising me for it all. It was quite something to see it all laid out in black and white. Whilst on the wards, I finished studying for my Honours degree in Psychology with the Open University and became a member of the British Psychological Society. I got a good degree and was anxious to study for my clinical psychology degree in Glasgow. I wanted to push myself very much as I loved learning new things, but Graham wouldn't hear of it. The children were still young and needed me, he said which was true enough, and because of my promotions I was paid reasonably well. Giving up my salary was not an option especially when my husband was not happy at work due to all the internal politics. He was unable to settle and never knew whether he might be better to leave and concentrate on something else, such as antiques.

I was also having to deal with the news coming from home where more tragedy and drama was to unfold. On 20th July 1974, the President of Cyprus – Makarios – was overthrown by a military coup and with the help of the United Nations, declared dead and smuggled out of the country. Nikos Sampson was appointed President; he stayed for eight days and when Turkey invaded Cyprus, he resigned from the presidency.

The invasion was brutal and destructive and took place at the five-mile beach near my friend's parents' hotel. On landing at the beach, they decapitated everybody including the parents of my friends. I was devastated to hear the news. The Greek Cypriots, including my family, had to leave everything behind and run for their lives over the mountains to the southern part of Cyprus. All the young men had to join the Army to defend their country. It was an impossible and unequal fight. My brother left his newly started architecture practice to become a captain in the Cypriot Army, in charge of 100-200 men. He was fighting on the Green Line and in the mountains and for some time he couldn't be traced – I was very worried so contacted my MP at the time, Mr McArthur, and explained the situation, asking for his help. Within a couple of days, he phoned me to tell me that my brother had been found alive by the Red Cross. I was so grateful he was alive – most of his contemporaries and friends died during that terrible invasion and massacre.

Both Britain and Greece, the so-called guarantors of Cyprus independence, were no help. Turkey, the third guarantor, became the aggressor. Greece, which was under the Greek junta at the time, tried to help the Cypriot Greeks by sending four boats, claimed to be full of rubble rather than ammunition but these were intercepted and turned back midway. Nikos Sampson belonged to the EOKA guerrilla movement, the liberators turned traitors. EOKA had fought for independence from Britain and were later responsible for the coup d'état against Makarios. There were terrible consequences of that day, rivers of blood during the invasion, tragedy and misery. We lost many friends, two houses, desirable plots of land, lemon groves, orchards and so much more.

The invasion was very traumatic when it happened and all I could do was watch the BBC news. I had terrible dreams of bombs and fire every night. Despo my sister, raced to Karavas to get our mother and made her flee with just the clothes on her back. It was horrific, but at least she escaped with her loved ones unlike many people we knew who were decapitated in cold blood.

My people became refugees, my aunt and her husband were herded up with others and forced to trek over the Pentadaktylos mountains to Nicosia. That was the end of my home, the homes of my friends, and of my childhood forever. There would be no more swims in the secluded bays, no more climbing on the Pentadaktylos mountains to gather flowers and smell the thyme and camomile bushes or visit the chapel of St George. I still miss everything very badly; the beautiful aroma of the lemon tree blossom still lingers in my brain. Yet another chapter was now closed. Scotland was now my home in every way.

Chapter Eighteen

The years rolled on by. Sophie our youngest was nearly five and ready for school. The girls and I were happy in Corsie Avenue, but not so Graham. He was anxious to leave academia for good and started an antique business as he was not happy at work; he was desperate to move out into the country so that he could grow his own produce and become self-sufficient. A 1750s Georgian manse came on the market, six miles out of Perth, with five acres of land and many outbuildings. The manse was enormous with lots of rooms, nooks and crannies. It had been empty for over a year and was in absolute ruins with the long upstairs corridor covered in bird droppings. It attracted a great deal of interest due to its potential and proximity to Perth: according to the old lady in the cottage opposite, there were a hundred and four viewers. We managed to buy it by the skin of our teeth but didn't have a penny left for anything else. It needed to be completely gutted and renovated, but it would be worth it as it was right in the heart of the country with the most amazing views from every aspect. There were mature yew and copper beech trees lining the long drive, even an orchard in one of the walled gardens. There was a well in the quaint two-storey washhouse and trout in a burn at the back of the house at the end of our wood.

However, it took a long time to restore. Any professional help was kept to a minimum as we didn't have the money. Graham taught himself more or less all the trades but it was all terribly slow. We all had to move to the second floor where the temporary kitchen was arranged. Some of the walls had to come down and the whole heating system replaced as it was badly leaking. All the ground floor had to be dug out before it was replaced due to rising damp, and the walls had to be specially treated because of the woodworm. Our friends thought we were crazy to undertake such a big task, telling us that we had bitten off more than we could chew. They were right as the next twenty-five years were to be spent in rubble and dust.

The winters out in the country were bitterly cold – we put in a Rayburn stove and huddled around it together in the kitchen for warmth. The beautiful countryside we had first seen in summer was transformed into a bleak expanse of fields and farms full of wind. There was a severe cold wave lasting for seven or eight weeks, the temperatures plummeted to -20 degrees Celsius. We had burst pipes everywhere and it was completely miserable. There was a leaky roof just above one of the girls' beds. The local farmer, Norman Strang, came to help us that night. He was a very pleasant good neighbour.

There were occasions when I opened the door to let the dog out and the snow was up to my eyes! Our black and white collie, Brax, would look up at me as if to point out to me that there was no way out! He was a highly intelligent dog but unfortunately, he loved to chase sheep. Many a time he would get involved in fights with Farmer Norman's dog and invariably we had to intervene before there was a tragic end. It wasn't easy. Brax eventually decided that young children were his competitors and enemies, so he selectively decided to nip them. Graham phoned me whilst working at the hospital one day and said that Brax had bitten a child and had to be put down. I was heartbroken.

I went to Cyprus that summer, to Protaras for a holiday, with my youngest daughter, Sophie. I desperately needed a break. We were sitting on the veranda of a restaurant, overlooking the blue Mediterranean Sea and watching the sun going down having just finished a lovely dinner, when we remembered Brax and tears started to flow down our faces. The proprietor was concerned, he offered us a couple of drinks on the house asking if everything was alright. It is very hard to get over the loss of a beloved pet.

We went back to Cyprus with the family many years later when Moina was married to Steven, Fiona was divorced, and Sophie was still married to Martin. The border regulations had changed then and one could visit the northern part as a tourist from abroad (but not from Cyprus). Nowadays it is slightly different in that a Greek-Cypriot with a visa can stay in a hotel for a couple of days. I was desperate to visit my home and my old town of Karavas, and although very frightening we decided to go.

When filling in the visa I said I was Scottish. I was careful not to talk and I made sure the others were around me so that I wouldn't be spotted. When on the other side, we hired a taxi as we were not allowed to bring our own car across the Green Line. I remember sitting next to the Turkish driver who realised, I think, that I was a local. He said to break the silence that he came from Paphos, so was the other way around, a Turk who was born in Paphos and he could now not go back as it was all Greek. He understood my situation and I his.

Going through the checkpoint was rather like entering Berlin, with soldiers with guns everywhere. The taxi took us to Karavas where my childhood home was and which I very much wanted to show to the girls. I remember walking up the street towards the long drive leading to the house.

We knocked on the door and Graham said in English, to the Turkish woman who came to the door 'We used to know the people who lived here. I have a lot of memories about the place – do you think we could have a look around?'

'Yes,' she said. 'That is fine.'

'Do you mind if we go to the back of the house?' asked Graham.

Again, she said that would be fine.

The hall was wide and long, the room where my father's body had been held so many years ago. Doors radiated to the other rooms and as I walked in, I looked from side to side, thinking of the past. My heart was thumping. We went to the back door and into the first of the three yards. At the side of it, the big deep pond was still there where we used to have small black and red fish swimming amongst the water lilies. The fish now were frighteningly enormous. It was not pleasant to look at them, I didn't like to see them. I had to keep all of my emotions under control and not show how I was really feeling. She left us to wander, but I still had to be careful. I looked over the little wall which was originally covered with so many pots of flowers and into the immediate front garden. This used to be stunning with plants and trees, and stretching beyond were lemon and banana trees, with a big palm tree sitting at the side of the yard further down opposite the outside oven. The only thing that was left in the now dried up field was that palm tree. It looked so forlorn. A lush place was now no more than a desert, all the fruit was gone. There was nothing left. It was a wasteland, a symbol of what had been lost.

We used to export so many lemons, but there was no awareness of basic agricultural skills among the people who occupied the land, and an entire industry was lost. When I smell a lemon, or see a cyclamen, I am transported back to my childhood. In spring, when the lemon blossom bloomed, you would open the door and the smell would hit you like a wall of beauty. Cyprus paid for its position, it was just always so strategic that everybody wanted it.

Our visit was very emotional.   We were only there for an hour or two as no more was allowed. I never visited the house again, although I visited Vasilia where my mother had been a teacher, on another visit to Cyprus. There were so many places we were not allowed to go on that day, places that were full of Turkish soldiers, such as the monastery. I felt as if my whole childhood had been wiped out and stolen from me. I thought of all there had been, all of that life, the night I was crowned a beauty queen, the times I had run about so freely, now all gone, transformed into something else that I could barely recognise.

Back in Scotland, Graham started suffering from seasonal affective disorder in the winters to add to his anxiety and unhappiness. Everything came to a stop at the manse as he had no motivation or enthusiasm to proceed with the house restoration. I had become resigned to living in a builder's yard indefinitely. The situation was not getting any better at the college. He was anxious to leave academia for good and start an antiques business, although this was not viable as antiques had started declining in popularity. Family furniture stores and antique shops were closing as young people were more interested in inexpensive modern furniture rather than traditional styles, many of which were just too large for modern houses. Graham's mental health deteriorated, his depression was getting worse and he was heading for a mental breakdown. He was granted early retirement at the age of 51 and we sold one of the enclosed gardens with planning permission as we needed the money to pay for private school fees for one of our daughters.

As well as my full-time work as a deputy in the hospital in Perth, I decided to start my own private clinic. Very quickly, I was much in demand and people travelled to see me from miles around. It was extremely hard work as sometimes I would be taking clients until 9 pm after a full day of work at the hospital, looking after the family and putting up with all the home renovations such as walls being knocked down, new windows and a roof being put in, and constant dirt and destruction all around me. All the money I earned was being thrown into a bottomless pit.

Unfortunately, my husband was becoming more controlling and possessive. He had always had such tendencies, but they were increasing at this point in our lives. Just then, out of the blue, Peter, my childhood friend, came back into my life. He would phone me during my breaks and have long conversations. He wanted our families to become friends. Peter was married now, he lived in Surrey and owned a well-known Greek restaurant in London. When we visited Chrysoula during the summer, he organised a big party for me in his garden. All of his Greek Cypriot friends were invited, some of whom I knew already. The food was amazing, there was music and dancing but Peter couldn't really hide his feelings for me and my husband was fuming. Peter's poor wife was jealous too. He came up to Perth secretly to visit me and we were planning to meet up in Cyprus on one of my visits back home. The holiday meeting did not materialise as Graham's strong instinct warned him that not all was well, so he announced that he was coming with me literally as I was getting ready to go to the airport that morning. I wasn't able to warn Peter of the latest development and he was waiting for me at Larnaka airport in Cyprus. It was all very unpleasant and added to Graham's paranoia.

His jealousy was spilling over into my professional life too. I spent a great deal of time and energy in getting my psychology qualifications and wanted to put them to some use. My husband put a stop to following my clinical psychology study dreams as he had done in the past with many of my academic endeavours, so I decided to qualify in hypnotherapy as I could do that relatively locally and thought it wouldn't interfere with the family in any way. I attended a basic level course at Stirling University and, as I found this very interesting, proceeded to study for further courses for my intermediary in the Midlands and later for advanced courses. I used my newly acquired qualifications and skills to treat problems such as phobias, bad habits, anxiety and depression. I became a member of the Clinical and Experimental Society Clinical Hypnosis (for Psychologists) which later incorporated Dental and Medical Hypnosis. I found this branch of psychology very interesting and used it successfully alongside my private physiotherapy business.

A course relating to some hypnotherapy topic of interest was advertised, taking place in Sheffield. I applied to attend but when I happened to mention this to Peter on the phone, he was intent on coming up. It all ended up in another disaster. Graham followed me down and arrived at the hotel asking many questions. I was not sharing a room with Peter; the whole affair was platonic, and I couldn't see anything wrong with just being friends. That made no difference to my husband who was livid. I genuinely thought he was going to murder me when I got back home. I took to my bed after that for a few days, refusing to eat or drink. I thought starving myself would have been a good way to die as my life was becoming intolerable because of his behaviour. The more those around me tried to persuade me to have something to eat, the worse I became.

I wanted to end it all. I wasn't particularly in love with Peter, I just wanted him to be my friend. He was part of my early teenage years, part of my happier days, a nostalgia of some kind. I knew I was doing wrong; I was playing with fire. Some might say I was a puppet on a string, with somebody from above directing me here and there but I do not feel that there was any excuse for how Graham reacted.

The whole incident seems so odd considering I had always been such a strong-minded woman. In situations where it would have been easier to just give up and buckle under the pressure, I pressed on. Perhaps it was my way of rebelling – enough was enough. My life took a long time to get back to any normality and there were no further suggestions of anything developing with Peter at all. Maybe I had been attempting to relive my youth, who knows, but our life was never the same again.

Life went on at the manse despite the ongoing chaos. We mixed and socialised with the locals, we became friends with the neighbours, we had long, pleasant walks in the surrounding countryside and along the banks of the Schochie Burn, which flowed at the bottom of our wood at the back of the house. I was unsettled by what had happened and my reaction to it when I wanted life to be over, but I got on with things, I had to – I always had. Just when I was getting used to renovation, the dust and the rubble, Graham wanted to move back to Perth.

At the time, my youngest daughter, Sophie, had given birth to a beautiful little boy they called Jamie. He was always unsettled and before long it became evident that he was profoundly handicapped with both mental and physical disabilities. After much research and many tests, we discovered that he was afflicted by the same genetic disorder that had led to the death of my brothers and the condition of so many male members of my family. All of that loss, all of that heartbreak over God knows how many years, had been caused by something called ATRX Syndrome, the family curse which reared its head once again with little Jamie. It was yet another blow to our family.

The Manse was now too big for just Graham and me, despite the fact that I was running a large clinic on the premises. It was soon put on the market and although still unfinished, sold for a handsome amount. We actually sold before we could find a place to our liking, so we temporarily stayed at Kinnoull Hill Place, just waiting to find something more suitable. The move was horrendous. Graham had always been a terrible hoarder and we had to face up to this with the move. Two enormous removal vans were loading household things over a few days, the house we were moving into was much smaller and most items had to go into storage. It took three years to remodel our new house and garden. We added an en-suite, new kitchen, new windows and in the meantime, I carried on with my physiotherapy business, family responsibilities and my full-time job. Life was certainly not slowing down for me.

••••••••◄◖▷►••••••

Chapter Nineteen

Afew years passed by when phone calls started coming from Cyprus from my sister telling me that all was not well with Mama. Throughout the years she had various minor incidents of stroke, a pacemaker put in, and all the usual travails that befall old age. Her health was rapidly deteriorating so I took a week off work and went back with Graham. It was late on a Wednesday evening when we arrived in the hotel in Larnaca. We got up early in the morning and arranged the car rental before heading to Nicosia. Just then, my sister Despo rang.

'Maro,' she said. 'Mama just passed away.'

I was devastated.

'But Despo,' I said, 'I would only have taken thirty minutes to get there – could she not wait for me?'

'I know, Maro. Mama was well aware that you were coming but she thought it best to go before she saw you. She didn't want to see you in case you held her back which meant that you would be coming back for the funeral in no time at all – she knew how precious your time is to you.' Mama was always so considerate.

The next day we all visited Mama in the mortuary. I remember her lying there with no wrinkles on her face and looking so very calm. All the siblings queued up, one by one saying goodbye to her, their last goodbye. She was so serene, so resigned to death. It seemed to me like an apotheosis was happening in front of my own eyes. I kissed her on the forehead and touched her hand, there was no response – she was simply cold, so very cold. She accepted death calmly and inevitably like so many other evil happenings in her life and she had undoubtedly been through many. A child with learning difficulties, poor Sotiris, three of her boys dead, a husband murdered, divorces of all three of my sisters, my beautiful youngest sister Thea afflicted with MS in her early twenties, becoming a refugee due to the Turkish invasion and losing everything she possessed – and I believe one of her final regrets was letting me and Chrysoula come to Britain at such an early age. A few times she asked my forgiveness about that but my answer was always that there was nothing to forgive, in fact, completely the opposite as it was the best decision she had ever taken in her life.

The next day was the funeral. People are buried soon after their death in Cyprus, unlike in Britain, probably because it is a hot country. Masses of people turned up to pay their last respects and say goodbye. All the refugees from Karavas and the surrounding areas, in fact, everybody who had ever known or heard of her family was there. They came from all over Cyprus where they settled after the Turkish invasion and the occupation of their homeland. There was a large overspill in the churchyard and the roads nearby. The Mayor of Karavas from before the invasion gave a long, wonderful speech about my mother, her humility, her quiet philanthropic work and her generosity to the poor, her accomplishments in life and much more. She was quite a special woman. After the funeral, everybody was queuing to shake hands and speak with me, explaining who they were. They knew me but I didn't know them. *How strange*, I said to myself, *were these the same people at my father's funeral, all those years ago?*

I often wondered if my mother had forgiven my father's killers. I think she probably did as she was a very religious woman and tried to follow Christian ethics – *forgive us our trespasses as we forgive those who trespass against us*. To have asked her this question would have been irrelevant and almost absurd. There comes a time at which one has to forgive others and also oneself. I believe it was Alexander McCall Smith who said that there is no point to keep on thinking about historical wrongs – to do so poisons and freezes relationships. It can be fatal for our souls, it clutters everything up, it distorts our thinking and behaviour towards those we must forgive and forget. It is very strange sometimes how we perceive the lives and situations of others. We may regard some people as lucky and privileged compared to ourselves – my mother perhaps thought that about me. She was a good woman and I cannot really see myself ever living up to her standard. And yet one day on one of my visits to her in Cyprus, a couple of years before her death, she said to me, 'Maro, I am so proud of you. If at any time I come back to this world, I would choose to come back just like you.'

'But why Mama?' I asked.

'Well,' she said, 'you have a perfect family, you have your husband, you are not divorced, you have a good profession helping people . . . and you have your looks.'

I tried to play it down at the time but many a time when I looked back, this is probably the greatest and best compliment I ever had.

We started to settle down again until a house at Mount Tabor Road came on the market (the house I am in now). My husband had his eye on it for some time. It is on a lovely site called Hollyhurst and is like an oasis in the middle of the city of Perth. There were extensive, mature gardens all around, but overgrown and unplanned, a bit like a jungle! Yet another project I thought, probably the same idea as all of the others Graham had tackled but thankfully not on the same scale. It certainly needed gutting, a new roof, window repairs, a new garage, a massive extension to mention just a few things. At least I didn't have a young family this time but, unfortunately, we were both becoming a lot older.

I still had my long-suffering physio and hypnotherapy patients who followed me about and kindly recommended me to lots of others. They were all good and understanding people, closing an eye to the heaps of rubbish all around. Unfortunately, as before, my husband wanted to do it all himself, but he was a lot older of course, and slower both physically and in terms of his motivation. A little while earlier I had given up my position as Deputy to the Superintendent and taken responsibility for the Gynaecological and Obstetric Department.

Seven years passed by with less than two thirds of the work on the house completed. There was still a great deal of rubbish lying around, lawns to be seeded, yards and walls to be built, a stove and boiler to be installed, and the inside of the house decorated. We were well on the way to this house perhaps, perhaps, being finished, when fate dealt a terrible blow.

On March 8th, 2017, I ran upstairs to wash my hair and shower. It must have been 9pm when I walked into the kitchen and found Graham flat out on the floor, lying on his side, motionless.

'What on earth are you doing there?' I asked him.

At first, I thought it was some kind of a joke but I very soon realised what had happened. He had suffered a brain haemorrhage, a massive stroke. I grabbed the phone and dialled 999. They answered immediately.

'Can I speak to him?' a woman's voice asked on the other end.

'How can you?' I replied. 'Believe me, I know for a fact that he has had a stroke. I am a physio and I know the symptoms.'

An ambulance came soon after. Graham was put on a stretcher and into the ambulance. There I was at the back of the ambulance with him, praying to God that it wouldn't be as bad as I envisaged. The young ambulance woman would now and again give me a quick glance. I knew the ambulance driver through my work at the hospital, but never before had I come across the woman. She was attentive to Graham and mentioned something about the rain. In the meantime, I contacted my three daughters with some difficulty, and they were all waiting for us at the hospital.

My husband was taken for a scan as the four of us waited patiently in the small, narrow waiting room, poised for the outcome but dreading it too. We were all silent, each of us given to our own private thoughts. The doctor eventually came out to speak to us.

'I'm very sorry,' he said, 'nothing can be done. The bleed to the brain is very extensive. All we can do is take him to the stroke unit.' It was getting very late by then – we were told to head home and visit him the next day. This was the end of an era and probably the beginning of the final chapter. The words of Frank Sinatra rang through my head – *and now the end is near, and so I face the final curtain. My friend, I'll say it clear, I'll state my case, of which I'm certain. I've lived a life that's full, I've travelled each and every highway, but more, much more than this, I did it my way.* How true this verse was to my husband, he was determined and possessive and that's how he managed to win me in the first place. He was stubborn, he loved me in his own way, he loved his family a lot but most of all he loved Scotland. He had a passion for this country from the moment I met him and I sometimes felt it was greater than anything else.

Graham stayed in the rehabilitation unit for the next four months. He was being fed through a nasogastric tube passed through the nose and down into the stomach since he had swallowing problems (dysphagia). He also lacked the ability to communicate (aphasia), he couldn't speak, write or understand either verbal or written language, and of course he completely lost the function of the right-hand side of his body which meant that he couldn't walk even a single step, or move and he didn't have the function of his right hand or arm.

I visited him every day during those four months. I knew some of the nursing staff and physios and they were excellent but there was only a certain amount they could do under the circumstances. Graham was in a very bad way. On my first visit, on my way out, one of the older nurses I knew stopped to speak to me.

'I'm so sorry, Maria' she said, 'A stroke is such a cruel thing.'

She could not have spoken a truer word.

I continued with my private patients who were, ironically, providing me with some sort of therapy. At the same time, I pursued the renovation of the house. I hired a big skip for all the piles of rubbish lying about and got an army of experts to finish what was left, especially the gardens and extensive paving. For the inside, I got an excellent odd-job man who worked for weeks, doing the painting and various repairs. More was achieved in those months than had been done in seven years. One of the most difficult things I had to do was sell Graham's De Dion 1902 veteran car. He loved that car and had originally gone to Canada to get it, just a pile of scrap metal which he had lovingly restored, often to the detriment of household renovations. A year or so before his stroke, he fulfilled a lifelong ambition, the London to Brighton veteran car run. I was in tears when I saw the car being carried out of the gate by the new owner. However, my husband would never have been able to enjoy it now and it had to go.

Eventually the day came for Graham to be discharged. The medical team strongly advised me that he should go into a care home. It was suggested that a feeding tube should be placed through the abdominal wall and into the stomach (PEG) but I rejected their advice. Despite his little cognitive understanding, Graham was adamant that he would be going home, so I went along with him since we had the right premises.

I completely underestimated the difficulties which lay ahead. Apart from the feeding problem, he couldn't attend to any of his own needs, he couldn't transfer without a lot of help, or even interact. He was completely dependent on other people. Nor were we given any hope. I was in a terrible panic when, on the first day, I managed to put him in the car with some help and bring him home. He was on powdered drinks which were out of stock at the pharmacy and on very soft foods which, on the first day, I had to get from Crieff, seventeen miles away, when he was sleeping in the passenger seat and in a bad way. I had great difficulty transferring him into the car despite my physio skills and even finding the store where I could collect the food.

Another big problem was the day and night catheters and the bladder bag. Although I had worked in hospitals for years, I had no idea of this aspect of things which was more of a nursing issue. I was in a desperate state, but I carried on. It was a steep learning curve. I had no carers to attend to him since there was some misunderstanding with the agency. No one would start for another two or three weeks. My former son-in-law, Martin, very kindly let me have one of Jamie's carers temporarily. This was a great help and I won't easily forget his kindness because it meant he had to look after Jamie a lot more himself.

Despite the odds, I managed. I have always been a fighter, but I was emotionally and physically drained by this. It took three years, but our situation did improve a little thanks to my physio skills. Graham got to the stage where, somehow, he could transfer and take some steps with a quadruped stick and someone's help, albeit with great difficulty. He could only do this inside the house, not outdoors. Most of his needs were managed with the help of carers who visited us four times a day. His cognitive ability started to improve somewhat during the last year or so of his life and the same with his speech. It was a great deal of effort on his part and mostly due to his sheer determination which still, despite his massive brain haemorrhage, prevailed. However, he became more demanding, and probably more frustrated no doubt, because he expected more from us all. I didn't think that there would be any improvement in his condition but, despite this, he always said he wanted to carry on living. When Covid-19 came into all of our lives, he was terrified and constantly said he didn't want to die.

The medical team, who looked after him in the stroke unit, the doctors and nurses, assigned him to an old people's home, declaring him a hopeless case but I did all I could for him and rarely rested. They would never have believed that Graham, in relative terms, could have done as well as he did but, of course, they were probably not as aware of his determination as I was.

I called an end to my physio business, a decision helped by lockdown, and officially retired. When times were hard with Graham, I would walk from our house up to the summit of Kinnoull Hill. This was, and still is, my place of refuge and I walk this circular route at least once a day. It is not exactly a replacement for Pentadactylos, the mountain overlooking my home in Karavas, but it has its own character and beauty, looking over the meandering River Tay down below in the valley. A perfect setting. I was also lucky to have such a lovely family and very good friends around me, and I did reach a place of contentment even with the demands from Graham. After all, he had always placed demands on me, and these were just different ones, of old age and illness.

Sadly, Graham's less attractive traits became even more obvious and accentuated after the stroke, which I believe often happens to those who suffer this horrible condition. He had invested his money in various banks before he became ill, and he was almost obsessed with accumulating funds. He would complain over every penny I spent (despite my good earnings), even when it was entirely necessary to buy whatever I purchased. One of the places which held quite a lot of his savings was the Skipton Bank. This was largely from the sale of Moneydie Manse and it was all under his name.

When Graham was very unwell with the stroke, he persuaded his carer to take him to the bank so that he could withdraw a large amount of money which I knew he could not have needed. I had no idea where the money went, whether he was giving it to someone or whether he was hiding it somewhere. I went into the bank and asked them to explain what was going on.

'Why are you allowing him to do this?' I enquired. 'Mr Norwell has had a massive brain haemorrhage and cannot reason properly.'

'It is his choice,' the teller informed me. 'If he is unable to make these decisions, then we will need a doctor's certificate to prove this is the case.'

It was yet another hurdle for me to jump over.

'Yes, we can do this,' I was told by someone at the surgery. 'It will cost £100.'

'Will the doctor have to tell Graham that the visit is to access his capacity?' I asked.

'Of course,' they replied.

'Then it is a waste of time,' I sighed. 'The doctor will be shown the door in no uncertain manner.'

I went back to the bank who insisted again that there was nothing they could do. My ill, dependent, physically fragile and mentally unsure husband was perceived by them as having full capacity. I could not understand this at all. Why were they indulging these dreadful decisions and why were there no safety measures in place to stop such withdrawals being made by customers who were clearly in no fit state to decide such things?

Undaunted, I asked if they could put me in touch with someone at their Head Office. Thankfully, after I made it very clear that I needed to talk to someone who had the authority to actually do something, I was allowed to talk to the lady in charge at the head office, who understood the situation. She asked the staff at the Skipton Perth branch to only allow Graham to have £50 per week out of the account.

The following week, yet again Graham visited the bank with his carer. When he returned home, aware of the restrictions which had been placed on his money, he was furious. He launched himself at me, grabbing at my upper arm – he still had much more physical strength than I anticipated and I had always been very slender. I ran out of the house, terrified, and called my daughter to come immediately. She spent a long time trying to get Graham to see sense but he was extremely angry and I was frightened that he might attack me again.

These were such difficult times. Strokes vary in their degree and severity – Graham was dealt a very bad one. Until it happened, he was a man with boundless energy. He was so active and interested in many issues, from antiques to vintage cars, house renovations or politics. He had been fanatical about Scottish independence throughout his adult life, even being asked to stand as a candidate in Inverness by the SNP – in fact, the Conservatives asked him to stand too! He rejected both offers for some reason. Graham had loved to discuss and debate current affairs, local, national and international politics, and I truly missed these discussions once he became ill. He had been a man with such wide interests and a remarkable intellectual capacity, he had enjoyed speaking to a broad range of people and always worked at being liked by others. His eloquence was such that he could give a speech at the drop of a hat.

When we lived at the Manse, he'd had to fight the Eagle Star Insurance Company in order to avert a huge housing estate, the size of a village, from being built all around us. He contacted newspapers, spoke on the radio, gave speeches in village halls and much more. To everyone's astonishment, he won the case. That was the man I married.

After he had the stroke, all of this was gone. It was as if all of the branches had been cut from a tree, leaving only the stump, exposed. The after effects were severe and devastating, he was left with so many mental and physical deficiencies, a shadow of the man he had been. He was not the same person, but I tried to think about the man he had been. I probably married him because of his persistence and his go-ahead attitude, his intelligence and the way he could talk to anyone about anything. That may have changed somewhat over the years, but what he was at the end was very unfair. When we first met, I was a little quiet and shy, I liked someone to do the talking for me as I never considered myself terribly chatty – now I would have to be Graham's voice too.

As I watched his intellectual capacity crumble, I could have wept at the thought of all those degrees, effort and learning fading to nothing. He was no longer a free and active member of society, he was a prisoner in his own body. Graham became rigid in his thinking obsessed with time and money, constantly clock watching.

He was frustrated, only interested in himself and became emotionally detached from the family. With his obsession with the clock, there was nothing else in his life. Graham had often been a hard man to live with, but there had been good times – both of us were robbed of so much by this horrible situation.

We lived like that for four years. Graham refused to even go for a few days respite throughout that time. I was exhausted on every level. It took its toll, each day was like an imprisonment for both of us. I tried to keep some of my independence but no matter if I managed to get out for an hour or two, I had to come back, always. On those few occasions when I did escape, Graham was constantly in the back of my mind, I felt guilty, but I also needed those glimpses of the world. I will admit that there was a time when I wished for him to just slip away. He was suffering. Latterly he wouldn't eat or drink, he was wasting away in front of my eyes. I hated that I was wishing the end upon him. It felt so wrong and yet I knew there was no other way for this to resolve itself, there would be no miracle. During those years, he showed no love for me, he became sterile in his emotions. There was never a moment when he demonstrated what we had been through, the many moments in which there had been a loving relationship. He expected me to be there no matter what, with never a word of thanks or a gentle touch of his hand on mine. In fact, he often treated me like the enemy. A glimmer of sweetness, a tiny gesture of love and affection would have meant the world to me, but it wasn't to be. It was indeed a cruel illness.

He became completely dependent and at odds with everything, including me and the carers. As I write my story, reflecting on everything, there seems so much to consider. I did love him, but he was a difficult man. I tried so hard to do something with my life and I wonder how much more I would have achieved if I was given a little more support.

I can recall a buzzard sitting on a branch of the tall trees at the end of the garden, month after month, watching Graham in the garden when his health was good. It disappeared for a while but came back when Graham became ill. I would see the bird every day but on the same day Graham died, the bird disappeared again and I have never seen it since. It makes me wonder, but perhaps that is my superstitious mind, the influence of my background. I think that Graham had more than thirty years of getting what he wanted. He retired at 52 and died at 85, and for each of those days, he was his own boss. If he got up in the morning and didn't want to do something, he wouldn't do it. If he had a notion for something else, he would follow that notion. He was still not happy. I could not indulge myself in that way, I had commitments and responsibilities. I always had so much to do but not a great deal of time for me.

I say that I lived in rubble and dust for twenty-five years, but actually, I have lived in it for all of my life. I had to emerge from rubble on so many occasions. And I did. I always did.

What I came from, what runs through my blood, has affected everyone. I'm not alone in that. I have had to grow and flourish in many different environments with my background dormant and often not permitted to affect me, I had to keep things under control. I had to conform, I had to adapt.

I always wanted people to recognise what I was capable of. These are hard things to look back on but I know that, right from the beginning, I wanted to lead; even thinking of just taking the children from one school to another makes me remember the feeling of being in charge and how much I liked it. Is it a personality trait? Perhaps. I always wanted to be a leader rather than a follower.

Maybe within such a big family everyone needs to find their place and I wonder if that was what drove me all my life – I was second born and perhaps I desperately wanted to be first. Chrysoula was older and the first grandchild so everyone gave her attention. She was competitive in everything in life, she wanted to be standing in front and I wanted that too, maybe we both inherited the same genes although, she is different to me in every way. She flared up quickly, I was one to sit back, and think about things to the extent that people believe I was easy going. I don't think I am in a real sense. I always want to strive and achieve and find a way and plan, and I don't really know where that comes from. I think my mother had this confident air with her and my father was able to deal with so many businesses and people, rich and of great status, lots of ladies and gentlemen sought him out and he was comfortable in their company. Maybe just being around that added to who I am. As I trained in psychology, I know that a combination of nature and nurture is behind every individual and their ways. It is indeed a mixture and that was clearly the case for me.

Chapter Twenty

Many years have passed since that stormy winter night of 30th January 1957. I suppose in some ways I have forgiven my father's killers, but never have I forgotten the injustice and suffering to my family brought about by their actions. I have to trust that they will be held to account by a higher power because they certainly never had to account to any court on earth.

A couple of years ago, my brother came across a former high-ranking EOKA leader who divulged to him that my father was unjustifiably wronged – something we knew all along, but it is still helpful to have it confirmed.

I am now at a stage of my life where I reflect on what has gone before. I think that I was born into a family who wanted to achieve a great deal. Despite my father's murder, despite everything that happened to Cyprus and all we lost, we all made something of our lives. For many in the family, a life that brought material wealth was a life well lived. For others, it was reputation and respect, being held in high esteem at least by their peers. Uncle Alexander and Auntie Ophelia always wanted to have more and be thought of as better than other people. Andreas, the cousin I was close to, always aimed for the top and thought he would achieve – and he did. If you believe in yourself and work hard, there is a strong likelihood that you will achieve what you want at least in material terms. Money makes money and also tends to marry it! My cousin, Nicos, became a mathematician and married a philologist from Athens and went back there to live a successful life in academia. Both Chrysoula and Despo obtained their PhDs. Chrysoula became a University lecturer and a psychotherapist, and Despo a Professor of Technology at Cyprus University. Andreas, my brother, became an architect in Cyprus and developed a thriving business.

Along with all the material success, there was illness, disability and tragic early deaths. Some of these adverse events were inherited and perhaps so was our drive to succeed.

We always had that work ethic, the drive to do things and I was a very physical child, which made for a good combination. For myself, the drive was a need to be acknowledged. Perhaps having the double disadvantage of being a girl and neither youngest nor oldest forged that need. The women on my mother's side and in her generation were unusual in that they were educated. Mama was very keen on academic qualifications and that was no doubt behind her sending me and my sister to England. In those days, women just didn't have much further education – most of them were kept at home and married someone wealthy if they were lucky. If you had a lot of dowry to give, you could end up marrying very well. If I had stayed, maybe I would have been a good catch but it would not have been the independent life that I craved.

Looking back, I can see how important external affirmation was to me. I wanted to be known as good at things – my school, my education, my job, as a mother, as a wife. I wanted to please all my extended family – and myself. I wasn't weak or meek, I was strong. I came across a lot of people during my psychology studies and when practising hypnotherapy and those who wanted to please other people all the time – this made me want to scream *stop it, please yourself!*

What made me 'me' was what I wanted and what I perceived other people would respect me fore. I loved to receive a prize, to have people applauding but I couldn't win everything. I hated coming second but I was not brilliant at everything, and I eventually accepted that. After all, life is not a competition with a single winner.

The loss of Papa pushed me to make something of my life, knowing that the fire of life could be extinguished all too easily, but Mama was a big part of my drive too. I became who I am because of them and because of me.

I have lived a long time and had many lives – the one in Cyprus, the one in England, the one in Scotland. I was a different person in each one. I have had a life well-lived, but I could have had a very different one if I had stayed in Karavas. I see my sister or brother and the way they live in Nicosia, a way which has its advantages, but I don't know if it would have been for me. If I had married well and been happy with my husband, I would have been alright, but I don't think I could have settled to a life of dependence, no matter how luxurious.   who can tell what will happen if you take a different path, or even one single different step?

People often comment on the difference between my lives – where I began and where I ended up. They think of the weather, but it is more than that. They often talk about the sun being wonderful and Scotland being terrible in that respect, but a clear sky and warm skin is not the be all and end all. Happiness does not care about the weather and is more important to feel that you have lived well, achieving all you could under the circumstances, and to have known love.

Would I have stayed if things had not changed? It depends. Many Cypriots went to other countries anyway, so I may very well have followed any husband I married there. I had seen my mother and grandmother break the rules to some extent – my mother with education, my grandmother by living the way she wanted to as an independent businesswoman – but there would always have been the pattern of following a husband wherever he went, even if I had my own decisions to make within that relationship. I had always seen that men had the power, but women could have more subtle influence. Papa's personality had always been strong but Mama had her own quiet way of achieving what she wanted and that was something I had to consider when my own husband decided that life was not happening in the way he wanted. When he took time off from me and our family, perhaps I could have argued, perhaps I could have said it was not right, but instead I preferred to see what I could do for myself and my girls.

I look back and see that Graham often lived the life of a single man. I was always in the role of wife and mother as well as a breadwinner. Many a time I considered divorcing him but it was important to me that my girls had a father in their lives so I put my head down and carried on. My father had always been demanding and controlling. Perhaps I had absorbed that as the prototype of relationships: father laying down the law, making lists and feeling in command while the mother appeared to be secondary but actually ran her life and household as she wished, exercising subtle control.

Chrysoula is a psychotherapist now, as well as my admired big sister. She says that I have become a great deal softer since my younger days. She thought I had been a bit of a monster as a child but my edges were rubbed off during the adulthood. Looking back at the chubby little girl living in paradise who knew how to get what she wanted and refused to do what she didn't want, I realise that she is probably right. Papa would refer to Chrysoula as the 'Spirit of Contradiction' but that term could apply equally to him and our mother. She says that I was always compassionate and a good listener and that has served me well throughout my life. 'We both concentrated on the challenges of survival and getting through whatever came across. Life just unfolded and we did not plan for the future. We both had to become more accepting and accommodating.' She also pointed out that we both ended up marrying clever and controlling men which was certainly true. Despo remembers that Mama always said when I got something in my mind, I would do it. Nothing could stop me and that was true and it was the reason that I had a good few arguments with Graham.

I have had a lot to overcome and there have been many obstacles, but I have played the hand I was given. No-one's life is a bed of roses and many lives have presented similar challenges, but not all have been blessed with the idyllic start in life that I had and which stood me in good stead. I hope that, despite all the challenges, I was able to give my children as good a start as my mother gave me. I often put my dreams on hold and just got on with it. It seems to me that this was just the way it was for women of my generation and before. When I was pushed from the path I wanted, I just found different things that I could achieve. Mama would always say, 'Nothing remains the same. No matter the adversity, there is always light at the end of the tunnel.'

You think more of your past as you age – you reminisce so much. Your memories are vivid, they are so clear despite being so far in the past. You become a foreigner in both countries, a part of you dies when you leave. Each time I visited Cyprus, I was a foreigner – you can never go back. My past had gone in so many ways. Scotland became my home country and I was adopted, but it took a while. I have been welcomed but, then again, I am the right sort of foreigner. My work helped then, I provided good things in my job, I made people better – I could be accepted.

When I think back to being a little girl, my strongest memory is sitting in winter by the burning open fire in the kitchen with my piggy bank getting all of the pennies out, all of my earnings. When I was about four and my sister was at school, in the brief period before Andreas was born, it was just me and Mama. She would be working around the place and I felt loved and secure.

Of all the scenes I recall, I did love the carefree life I had in Vasilia. It was only for a year but a year in a child's life is probably the equivalent of about five and it imprinted on me deeply. When I arrived in England, the overwhelming sense I had was that which had been was now gone. All I was interested in was how I faced the here and now. This was a new world for me. I don't suppose my life from that point was what I had expected it to be. It was conformist, it was smaller than I had imagined, but I had to survive, I had to keep pushing forward. I had to make the best out of it.

The last snapshot of my life is looking back on the woman I have been. Life is full of challenges and I have had as many as most. I think I've done not too badly, under the circumstances. I rose to all challenges and took them on, I got on with things and with life. There was no time really to sit back and say, 'I want a different life.' There are things I could have done better: none of us is perfect but I do think I tried. I have done my best. Maybe I was too accepting of being controlled sometimes, but life and fate put me into a relationship with someone whose personality made our marriage the way it was.

I wonder what would have happened if that day before my wedding I had decided that, no, I would not go ahead with it. I would stop the train; I would make my own way and not feel that I had to do things for other people? Of course, I will never know.

Eventually I did it, I got everything I ever wanted - a nice family, a career where I could help people and which I thoroughly enjoyed, my academic qualifications and a happy home. I also won the respect of people I admired. I'd always wanted and needed that external validation, the recognition and the feeling that people valued me. You may have noticed that I have never suffered from false modesty and I am not ashamed to own my aspirations.

I am happy in my house on the hill and have no plans to move, but if I had to, I would be fine. I have no profound sense of place, of being rooted or overly attached to the material things of life. I attribute this to the land of my birth and the understanding from a very young age that everything is transient and there are many things a person cannot control. Losing my school, my father and ultimately my family home established for me the importance of being self-sufficient and of people over things, even houses.

I have seen the darkness and the light, I have been thrown into the depths of despair but also enjoyed the heights of happiness. Perhaps I have come to the end of my rainbow. As I look back at that little girl called Maro, I tell her, *it has been a life of many colours and I am a woman I can be proud of. Strive to be who you want to be, and you will be content.* I have lived many lives and I have many memories. I reached the moon after all.

⚬—⚬≺◆≻⚬—⚬

Me and Chrysoula 2021

Me and my friend Bobby 2016

Graham, May 2020

Graham in his veteran car

Moneydie Manse

Acknowledgements

Thank you to my family and daughters for all the support while writing this book. To my sisters for proof reading, multiple times, along with Judy, a cousin of my husband. A special thanks to my long-suffering friends for listening to me talk about this book for so long, especially Breeda. I would also like to thank my friend Morag, who listened carefully and provided suggestions to the structure of my story.

Thank you all.